simply shrimp

with 80 globally inspired recipes

Published in 2007 by Stewart, Tabori & Chang
An imprint of Harry N. Abrams, Inc.

Library of Congress Cataloging-in-Publication Data

Peterson, James.
Simply shrimp:with 80 globally inspired recipes /
James Peterson.
    p. cm.
Includes index.
ISBN-13: 978-1-58479-585-8
1. Cookery (Shrimp) I. Title.

TX754.S58P47 2007
641.6'95--dc22

2006022624

Editor: Christine Gardner
Designer: LeAnna Weller Smith
Production Manager: Alexis Mentor

The text of this book was composed in AA DTLNobelIT.

Printed and bound in China
10 9 8 7 6 5 4 3 2 1

HNA
harry n. abrams, inc.
a subsidiary of La Martinière Groupe
115 West 18th Street
New York, NY 10011
www.hnabooks.com

simply shrimp

with 80 globally inspired recipes

James Peterson

stewart tabori & chang • new york

contents

introduction

IN MY EARLY TEENS MY FATHER, A CAREER NAVAL officer, went back to school to get his degree in business and would lecture us, at dinner, about the great economists. When I learned about Malthus I began to lay awake at night, pondering the exponential growth of humanity and the arithmetic growth of agriculture. I would imagine our quiet suburban neighborhood turned into a nightmarish Kolkata, our family battling with the neighbors over scraps of food. By the year 2000 the world was to be a teeming mass of humanity with nothing to eat and no space to move. Thankfully, my horrible vision did not come to pass. At that time, few would have anticipated the technological advances in husbandry, agriculture, and aquaculture that have made the land and sea much more productive and most foods relatively cheap.

Unfortunately, many of these inexpensively produced foods don't have the flavor of their predecessors. The flavor of shrimp varies enormously depending on whether it's wild or farmed, and if it is farmed how that's done, and finally how it's handled once harvested. Some shrimp ends up getting frozen and refrozen to the point where it has no flavor. So in tandem with the new productivity and abun-

dance is a countertrend. Those of us who can afford it seek out low-yielding heirloom tomatoes, archaic pork, free-range poultry, and grass-fed beef. Some of us can pay for long-lost flavors while others eat inexpensive versions of the original. There is abundant mass-produced food to keep us from going hungry and newly discovered "old" foods to seduce our palates.

Two decades ago, virtually all shrimp was wild. There wasn't much to go around and it was expensive—about as much as lobster. Now, because most shrimp is farmed, both wild and farmed shrimp have become relatively cheap. We have an abundance of what was once a luxury and are again confronted with a gastronomic schism between an inexpensive, farmed product and the rare gift of nature. As buyers become more discerning and ask for wild shrimp or high-quality farmed shrimp, some farmed shrimp may actually go down in price. This is just as well since the low price of shrimp now risks driving shrimp fishermen out of business. Unlike twenty years ago, we have a choice.

One reliable cook's axiom is that the finer the ingredients, the more simple should be the cooking. If you find wild Gulf shrimp, preferably with the heads on, don't make an elaborate dish with all kinds of competing flavors. Cook the shrimp simply—sauté it, grill it, or smoke it, so its flavor comes through—or prepare a dish that makes use of the heads to reinforce the shrimp's flavor. If the shrimp is less flavorful, use it as a foil for more adventurous dishes, such as many of the recipes in this book that have been inspired by Mexican, Indian, and Thai cooking.

Now about the heads. Most of us forget that like chickens, ducks, and other animals, shrimp have heads—or more accurately, thoraxes. The thoraxes have eyes, little flippers, legs, and various paraphernalia to help the shrimp get around. While it seems that some of these anatomical details give people the whim-whams, it also happens that the heads contain roe and various innards— I won't go into the specifics—that are the most flavorful part of the shrimp. If you're eating whole head-on shrimp, twist the head off and suck out the juices and you'll see what I mean. If you don't want to serve your guests head-on shrimp, you may still want to buy head-on shrimp anyway—this may mean a special order at your local fish market or a trip to an Asian market—so you can use the heads

to add flavor to soups, stew dishes, or sauces. If you don't want to bother with the heads at the moment, save them and the shells in the freezer until you're feeling more ambitious.

The cuisines of the world fall into two camps: those that underline and reinforce the flavor of a particular food— the French are geniuses at this—and those that accent the food and bring it into relief by juxtaposing it with opposing flavors. You can also play the two sides by using both approaches. The best way to get at the flavor of shrimp is to cook the heads, grind them up in a food processor, and simmer them with water, sometimes with some cream added so the fat can draw out the shrimp's color and those flavors that are soluble only in fats. The resulting broth can become a soup or stew base or be boiled down to make a sauce. You can also use the heads and/or the shells to make bright orange Shrimp Butter (see page 183) and keep this butter in the freezer for whenever you want to add a shrimp or crustacean flavor to a soup, sauce, or stew.

While this book contains recipes both simple and elaborate, the actual cooking of shrimp is very simple in part because shrimp is done as soon as it's heated through, rarely longer than 3 or 4 minutes. To get it to retain the most flavor, cook it—boil or sauté it—in the shell. If you don't want your guests to grapple with peeling the shrimp or you want the shrimp to release its juices and flavor into a surrounding cooking liquid, peel it first. Whether you're cooking the shrimp with or without the shell, you can sauté it, grill it, smoke it, boil it (best if it's in the shell), or cook it directly in a stew, soup, or sauce. All the variations and recipes are about juxtaposing the shrimp with other textures and flavors, reinforcing the shrimp's flavor, or both.

Often, when I mention to people that I'm writing another cookbook, they ask, "How many recipes?" as if the number of recipes were the only measure of a cookbook's value. This book contains only eighty recipes, but they are the best examples of the way shrimp is cooked throughout the world and also in ways that are a result of my own imagination and experience. I'd rather arm readers with a dozen reliable recipes that they cook over and over and learn by heart than include lesser recipes in an effort to be exhaustive and to impress by quantity alone. I also care, here and in my other books, about teaching the reader how to cook. To do this I clarify the basic techniques—frying, sautéing, grilling, stewing, and others—and in a parallel way, familiarize the reader with the flavor groupings of the world's greatest cuisines. The clearest example of this kind of information is included in the chart on pages 98–99.

When readers understand how a particular food—in this case, shrimp—behaves when it's exposed to heat and understand its affinity for certain flavors, they will be free to invent and improvise according to what's on hand, the formality of the occasion, or just pure whim.

Most of the recipes in this book make the deveining of shrimp an option, not mandatory. I've eaten shrimp in many places in the world and have never seen it deveined except in the United States. If you're serving unpeeled shrimp, the choice to devein is left to the guests; otherwise the choice is yours. I suggest you devein a shrimp or two (see page 14 to learn how) and look at the little digestive tube. When shrimp were all wild, the tube was invariably filled with grit and was an unsightly black. Today, most farmed shrimp seem to be allowed to go hungry long enough that the tube is empty and there's no need to deal with it.

When I was in my early twenties, I decided to cook a special dinner for my roommates. When I paid for the $6-a-pound shrimp (about $50 in today's dollars) with food stamps, the cashier sneered and said, "What is this? Crabmeat?" I said "No, shrimp." She said, "That's worse." Nowadays I wouldn't embarrass myself. I have tried to provide here a versatile introduction to what was once a rare and exotic food reserved for special occasions or visits to a Chinese restaurant. But because shrimp has become easier to find and more affordable and appears in far more variety than it did a generation ago, it merits a collection of recipes and techniques such as this one to help us make it part of our regular diet. This book will introduce you to the essential methods for cooking shrimp and to a varied assortment of recipes derived from the world's greatest cuisines; it aims not only to teach you how to cook shrimp, but to discover a new palate of savory combinations appropriate for both daily meals and more adventurous forays into your kitchen.

How to Buy Shrimp

While there are hundreds of varieties of shrimp, most are so small that they're never marketed, except to those of us who have fish tanks. Of the dozen or so types of shrimp that we're likely to encounter, most are so-called tropical shrimp (from the species *Peneidae*) found in warm water in the Gulf of Mexico, in parts of South America, and in Asia. Occasionally we may see somewhat smaller northern shrimp from the species *Pandalidae* that are harvested from Greenland as far south as Maine. These shrimp are easy to spot because they're bright red when raw; they are sometimes served raw in sushi bars. Freshwater shrimp, which have long, blue front legs, are occasionally found wild but are mostly farmed, largely in the Caribbean. Rock shrimp are an entirely different species, caught off the coast of Florida, and because their shells are difficult to remove, they are sold already out of the shell.

A generation ago all shrimp were caught in the wild and were almost as expensive as crabmeat, but today most are farmed in various parts of the world, resulting in much lower prices for all shrimp, including wild shrimp. While each type of shrimp has its own flavor nuances, the most important consistent guarantee of a full, nutty flavor is that the shrimp be wild rather than farmed. Farmed shrimp can be as flavorful as wild shrimp—when the ponds are large enough ecosystems form naturally, giving farmed shrimp the same complex flavor as that of wild shrimp—it's just harder to be certain of its quality. How do you know what you're getting? Unfortunately a shrimp looks the same whether it is full of flavor or not; the only way to be sure is to trust your fish store.

Strangely, most Americans have never seen a whole shrimp. Americans are the only people in the world who don't seem to want to be reminded that they're eating a living sea creature with a head, antennae, and various flippers and swimming paraphernalia. The only way to get shrimp with the heads on is to order them ahead of time or buy them in an Asian market. Unless the shrimp are very small the head isn't usually eaten but it is sucked on since it's the tastiest part of the shrimp. It's also very useful for making flavorful soups, stews, and sauces, for which you'd otherwise need shells from an enormous number of headless shrimp.

Shrimp Varieties

WARM WATER SHRIMP

Most species of warm water shrimp are named after a color—white, pink, brown, or blue—which often has little to do with their actual color; white shrimp can be brown, brown shrimp pink, etc.

WHITE SHRIMP: There are five kinds of white shrimp.
Gulf White Shrimp: These are harvested in the Gulf of Mexico as well as along the east coast of the United States as far north as North Carolina, and are among the tastiest shrimp.
West Coast White Shrimp: These shrimp live in the wild along the coasts of South and Central America and are usually labeled according to where they've been caught or farmed. Farmed Ecuadorian shrimp is an especially common and relatively inexpensive type of West Coast white shrimp.
Central American White Shrimp: Don't confuse these shrimp, which are usually caught in the wild and have a full flavor, with the more commonly farmed West Coast white shrimp.
Chinese White Shrimp: These are both farmed and caught in the wild off the coast of China. The best quality are

sometimes labeled "seaswallow" and the next best quality "billow." Most that are found in American markets have been farmed.

Indian White Shrimp: Huge numbers of these shrimp, which are farmed and harvested all over Asia, are marketed throughout the world.

PINK SHRIMP (sometimes called Mexican pink shrimp): These are among the most flavorful shrimp when caught in their wild habitats, the Gulf of Mexico and the southern Atlantic coast of the United States. They are sometimes sold farmed, so it's important to know what you're getting.

BROWN SHRIMP: Often caught in the wild, these shrimp are found from North Carolina to the Gulf of Mexico. Brown shrimp were long considered inferior to pink or white shrimp, but now that so much shrimp is farmed, wild brown shrimp is comparatively very satisfying. The shell is usually brownish and has a little groove near the tail.

TIGER SHRIMP (sometimes called black tiger shrimp): This is one species of shrimp that is easy to identify—they have black stripes. Tiger shrimp are harvested extensively throughout Asia and are found wild in the Indo-Pacific area. Most tiger shrimp sold in the United States have been farmed and don't have a whole lot of flavor.

BLUE SHRIMP: Just to add to the confusion, these are sometimes called Mexican whites or West Coast whites. They are both farmed and caught in the wild (on the Pacific side of Mexico) and sometimes have a blue tint on the shell.

COLD WATER SHRIMP

There are three major species of cold water shrimp, which are caught in the western United States along the coast of Alaska and as far south as Monterey, California, as well as in the east along the coast of Greenland and as far south as Maine.

NORTHERN PINK SHRIMP: These are easy to recognize because they're bright red when raw—unlike Mexican pink shrimp, which are pink or white. These shrimp are smaller than most Gulf shrimp.

GIANT SPOT SHRIMP: These are caught in the same parts of the world as northern pink shrimp but are usually larger, firmer, and more flavorful.

SIDESTRIPE SHRIMP: These are easy to spot because of the stripe along their sides. They are caught on the west coast from Alaska to Oregon.

ROCK SHRIMP: Because they're sold already shelled and are relatively inexpensive, these little shrimp are ideal for soups and stewy dishes. They're too small to grill.

FRESHWATER SHRIMP

These beautiful blue-tinted shrimp are farmed and tend to be quite expensive.

How Shrimp Is Sold

Most shrimp sold in fish markets are raw and headless, with the shell on. It's a good idea to avoid buying cooked shrimp, since some stores cook the shrimp that start to go bad. The sizes available are usually medium, large, and jumbo, but these terms aren't closely regulated and can be relatively meaningless. In the industry, shrimp is sold according to the number of shrimp per pound. Usually a range such as 26/30 means that there are that number of shrimp per pound. Very large shrimp are sometimes sold with a U, such as U15, meaning under 15 per pound. Tiny shrimp are sometimes sold with an O, for over, such as O100. Keep in mind that U16 shrimp would weigh 1 ounce each; U8 shrimp, 2 ounces; 30/34 (average 32), ½ ounce; etc.

Most shrimp arrives at the retailer in frozen boxes, usually weighing 5 pounds each, and is rarely found fresh. Because shrimp is frozen as soon as it's harvested, freezing it actually keeps it "fresher." The only risk is that the fish seller has left it thawed out too long in the display case. Shrimp that's been recently thawed should look shiny but with no signs of foam or froth and should smell like the ocean, not fishy. If you cook a lot of shrimp, the safest bet is to buy a whole 5-pound frozen box (with the size and origin of the shrimp clearly marked on the box) so that you know it's never been thawed. Shrimp is also sometimes sold IQF—individually quick frozen—in bags in the supermarket. This is convenient because you can keep a bag in the freezer and only take out as many as you need. You can make your own IQF shrimp by thawing a frozen block, spreading the shrimp on sheet pans so they're not touching, and refreezing them before putting them in bags.

Shrimp is sometimes dipped in a solution of sodium bisulfite, a commonly used preservative, to prevent melanosis—also called black spot—which stains the shell and sometimes the flesh as the shrimp deteriorates. Shrimp that's been peeled is sometimes dipped in sodium tripolyphosphate, in the same way as scallops, to prevent drip loss. The only way to avoid these chemicals is to insist on "additive-free" shrimp—you must trust your fish store—or to buy your shrimp in a block. Sodium tripolyphosphate sometimes gives a slippery feel or soapy taste to shrimp, while sodium bisulfite may give it a sandpapery feel.

How to Prepare and Cook Shrimp

Most recipes for shrimp call for deveining, the process of taking out the little intestine that runs the length of the shrimp and that's sometimes filled with grit. Now that much shrimp is farmed, there tends to be little if any grit so this process can be skipped for all but the most squeamish. (The United States is the only country where shrimp is deveined.)

Shrimp is always more flavorful when cooked in the shell, because the shell seals in the juices, so you can just boil shrimp in the shell and it will taste perfectly delicious. Sometimes, though, if you don't want your guests to work too hard, or you want the flavor of the shrimp to go into the surrounding liquid—such as a sauce or soup—you should peel the shrimp first. The shrimp shells (and heads if you are using shrimp with the heads still on) should be saved in the freezer; once you have a couple of quarts of shells, you can make a broth that can be used in soups and stew dishes.

Some cooks like to soak shrimp in brine, which helps plump it up and gives it more texture. Certain kinds of shrimp can benefit from this process, especially farmed shrimp that has been frozen and refrozen, which can render it pasty and soft.

WHAT ARE PRAWNS?

In some parts of the United States, and in other countries, shrimp, especially if they are large, are called prawns. Dublin Bay prawns are the only prawns that aren't shrimp but are instead what the Italians call *scampi* and the French call *langoustine*. It's unusual to see prawns for sale in the United States, although a variety from New Zealand, which look like miniature lobsters, has begun to appear here. Freshwater shrimp are often called prawns, and tiny wild shrimp, often used for shrimp cocktail, are called bay shrimp.

SHRIMP SIZES AND YIELDS

At each stage of cleaning and cooking, a shrimp gets smaller and yields less edible flesh. When calculating how much shrimp you need for a specific dish, the final size of the shrimp doesn't matter very much—you just need to adjust the cooking time by a minute or so according to size—but the total amount of shrimp after peeling will provide you with an easier way to figure out how much you need. Appetites vary, of course, but 6 to 8 ounces of shrimp after peeling but before cooking is about right for a main course, and about 4 ounces is enough for a first course. Here's a breakdown of a pound of shrimp:

1 pound raw shrimp with heads and shells = 0.6 pound (9 ounces) unpeeled headless shrimp

9 ounces unpeeled headless shrimp = 0.4 pound (7 ounces) peeled shrimp

7 ounces peeled shrimp = 6 ounces when cooked, or about 38 percent of the original weight of the original 1 pound raw shrimp with heads and shells

How to Peel Shrimp

A and B: If the shrimp have heads, twist them away from the tails and pull away.

C and D: With the concave part of the shrimp facing up, pull the shell away from both sides.

E: Continue opening up the shell and pulling it away until it detaches from the tail.

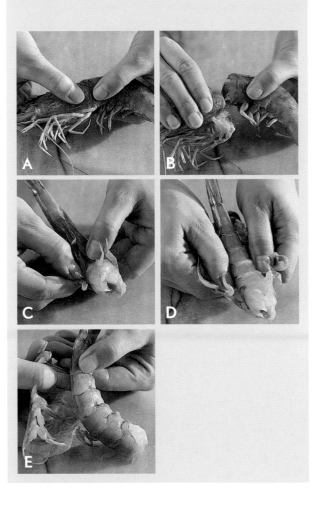

How to Devein Shrimp

A: Slide a knife along the outer, convex, side of the shrimp, cutting in about ⅛ inch.

B and C: Open up the slit you made with the knife to reveal the intestinal tube and pull it out.

D: Finished deveined shrimp.

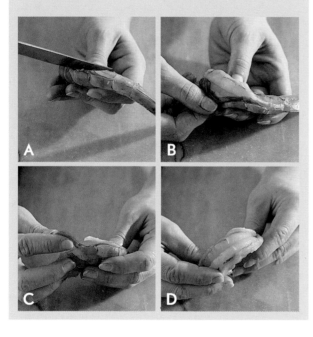

Hence, for a main course serving of 7 ounces, you need to buy 9 ounces of unpeeled shrimp without the heads, or a pound of shrimp with the heads and shells. For a first course serving, figure on about half as much. To calculate the number of shrimp per serving, you'll need to know the number size of the shrimp, since terms like large, extra large, and jumbo are vague. Here are some approximate amounts for various sizes:

Jumbo shrimp with heads weigh about 3 ounces each and so are about U5.

Jumbo shrimp without heads weigh about 2 ounces each and so are about U8.

Extra large shrimp with heads weigh about 2 ounces each and so are about U8.

Extra large shrimp without heads weigh about 1½ ounces each and so are about U10.

Large shrimp with heads weigh about 1½ ounces each and so are about U10.

Large shrimp without heads weigh about 1 ounce each and so are about U16.

Medium shrimp with heads weigh about 1 ounce each and so are about U16.

Medium shrimp without heads weigh ½ to ¾ ounce each and so are U24 to U32.

If you're starting out with headless shrimp, count on losing about one-fourth by weight when you peel them and one-fifth of that when you cook them, so that 1 pound of headless shrimp will actually give you 11 ounces of cooked shrimp. Sometimes it's easier to go by the number of shrimp rather than the weight. The larger the shrimp the more expensive they are (larger shrimp also tend to have more flavor), so unless you're serving the shrimp grilled or in some dramatic way, you can get by using smallish shrimp—it will just mean more peeling. If you buy very large shrimp, usually called jumbo (in the industry there are superjumbo, colossal, and supercolossal, but it's rare to see these in a fish store), count on fewer per serving. If you're in doubt about the size of the shrimp at the fish market, buy by the number:

SHRIMP REQUIRED FOR
ONE MAIN COURSE SERVING

1 pound head-on shrimp or 9 ounces headless shrimp gives 7 ounces of peeled shrimp (one serving). Here are approximate numbers of shrimp you'll need per main course serving:

4 jumbo, head on or headless

5 extra large, head on or headless

7 large, head on or headless

9 medium, head on or headless

SHRIMP REQUIRED FOR A LIGHT MAIN COURSE OR
FIRST COURSE SERVING (4 ounces peeled, headless)

2 jumbo, head on or headless

3 extra large, head on or headless

4 large, head on or headless

5 to 6 medium, head on or headless

BRINING

With a little forethought, you can improve the texture of shrimp by soaking it in brine for an hour or so. To make enough brine for 2 pounds of shrimp, dissolve 1 cup sea salt and ½ cup sugar in 2 cups of hot water. If you want to flavor the brine with herbs, bring it to a simmer, take it off the heat, and add a few sprigs of fresh thyme, tarragon, marjoram, or a little chopped fennel and let cool. While the brine is still warm, but not distinctly hot, add a tray of ice cubes. (If you skip this step and chill the brine in the refrigerator instead, compensate by diluting the brine with an extra cup of water. When the brine is well chilled, soak peeled shrimp for 20 to 40 minutes (20 minutes for medium shrimp, 40 for jumbo shrimp) and unpeeled shrimp for twice as long.

salads and cold dishes

Shrimp, Avocado, Bell Pepper, and Citrus Salad

MAKES: 4 generous first course or light main course servings

This salad is similar to the tomato salad on page 22 but also includes avocado, which contribute richness and that unmistakable buttery texture, and citrus fruits, which give it tang.

16 large shrimp

2 bell peppers, preferably one yellow and one red, charred, peeled, (see page 20), stemmed, seeded and cut into ⅛- to ¼-inch strips

4 navel oranges

2 grapefruits

4 thick slices bacon, cut crosswise into 1-inch-long, ¼-inch-wide strips (optional)

2 heads Belgian endive

2 ripe avocados, preferably Hass

¼ cup fresh lime juice (from about 2 limes) or more to taste

¼ cup extra virgin olive oil

2 jalapeño peppers, stemmed, seeded, and minced

1 small bunch parsley, large stems removed, leaves and small stems chopped fine

salt and pepper to taste

1. Cook the shrimp by plunging them in about 3 quarts of boiling water and boiling for 2 minutes. Drain in a colander and rinse with cold water. Peel the shrimp and, if you wish, devein them. Set aside.

2. Grate the zest off half of one of the oranges and reserve. Cut the oranges and grapefruits into skinless wedges (see photos, opposite) and reserve.

3. Cook the bacon in a small skillet over low to medium heat for about 10 minutes until the strips are crispy. Drain on paper towels. Cut the bottom half of each endive crosswise into ½-inch-thick slices. Within an hour of serving, peel the avocados and cut them into lengthwise wedges; you should get 12 wedges per avocado.

4. Gently toss the avocado wedges with the citrus fruits, the bacon, the endive slices and leaves, the pepper strips, the lime juice, the olive oil, the jalapeño chiles, the parsley, and the orange zest—reach under them in a bowl with your hands or two spoons and gently fold them over themselves. Season to taste with salt and pepper. To serve, arrange the fruit-avocado mixture on 4 chilled plates and place 4 large shrimp on each one.

How to Cut Citrus Fruits into Skinless Wedges

A: Slice off the two ends—the north and south poles—of the fruit just deep enough to see the flesh.

B and C: Place the fruit on one of the flat ends and cut away the peel with a paring knife, following the fruit's contours.

D: Cut along the membranes that separate each of the wedges. Cut just deep enough to reach the center of the orange.

E and F: Continue in this way, folding back the membranes as you go, until you've separated all the orange wedges from the pulpy membranes.

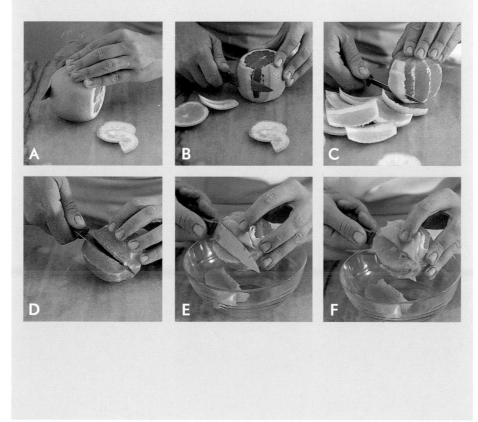

How to Peel Bell Peppers

There are three ways to go about peeling bell peppers. The usual method is to put the peppers directly over a high gas flame or to grill them over high heat for a couple of minutes on each side until the peel completely chars. Then, after letting the peppers cool, you just pull off the peel with your hands. To get rid of stubborn patches, scratch at them with a knife. This method also works well with the larger chile peppers, such as poblanos.

If you have an electric stove, turn it on high. Then make a rack for the peppers by bending down each end of a wire coat hanger, holding it as though it is actually hanging in front of you until the ends almost completely come together. The hanger then creates a 1/16- to 1/8-inch rack that you then place directly on the metal coils of the heated stove. Place the peppers on the hanger and rotate them as needed, until the whole pepper is completely charred. If the pepper starts to turn from black to white, you're overcharring it.

If you want perfectly bright peppers with none of the black staining that charring can cause, preheat the oven to 400°F and roast the peppers on a sheet pan for about 20 minutes, turning once after about 10 minutes. Turn the oven off with the peppers in it and don't open it for an hour. The skins will be loose and easy to pull off.

How to Peel and Dice Tomatoes

A: Plunge the tomatoes in boiling water for 15 seconds, drain in a colander, and immediately rinse with cold water. Pull away the peel with your fingers and a paring knife.

B: Cut a slice off the top or bottom of the tomatoes to help them stand on end.

C and D: With the tomato standing on end, cut away the outer pulp with a paring knife, following the contours of the tomato.

E: Cut the pulp into small strips, then slice into ¼-inch dice.

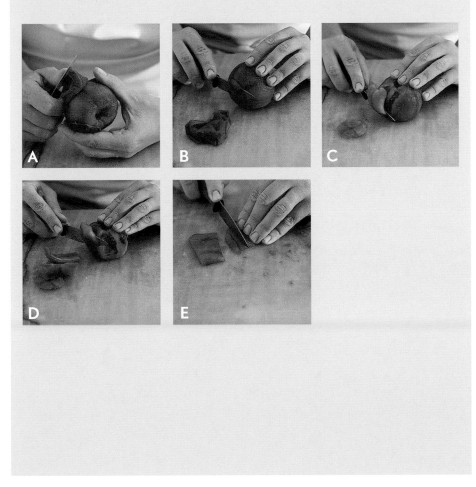

Shrimp, Heirloom Tomato, and Bell Pepper Salad

MAKES: 4 first course servings

16 large or extra large shrimp

10 tomatoes in a variety of colors and sizes

1 red bell pepper, charred, peeled (see page 20), stemmed, seeded, and cut into a ¼-inch or smaller dice

1 yellow bell pepper, charred, peeled (see page 20), stemmed, seeded and cut into a ¼-inch or smaller dice

⅓ cup extra virgin olive oil

3 tablespoons flavorful sherry wine or red wine vinegar

salt and pepper to taste

This salad is best in the late summer or early fall when many different colored tomatoes show up at farmers' markets. You can make it as formal or casual as you like by cutting the whole tomatoes into wedges, or by peeling and seeding them and, if you're being really elegant, cutting out the inside pulp. The salad will look very dramatic if you use a large variety of different colored tomatoes.

1. Cook the shrimp by plunging them in about 3 quarts of boiling water and boiling for 2 minutes for large shrimp and 3 minutes for extra large. Drain in a colander and rinse with cold water. Peel the shrimp and, if you wish, devein them. Set aside.

2. Cut the tomatoes into wedges or slices, or, if you choose, remove the skin and prepare slices as shown on page 21.

3. Toss the peppers with the tomatoes, oil, vinegar, salt, and pepper. Arrange the mixture on 4 chilled plates and place 4 large shrimp on each one.

Tropical Fruit, Avocado, and Grilled Shrimp Salad

MAKES: 10 first course or 6 main course servings

The combination of heat from chiles, smokiness from the grill, and the cool sweetness of tropical fruit makes this salad a hit. The trick is to prepare the basic salad ahead of time and then, at the very last minute, toss in the sizzling shrimp right off the grill. You'll notice if you have any of this left over—unlikely, but still—that the shrimp will have turned to mush by morning. This is because the protease enzymes in the fruit will break down the proteins in the shrimp.

1. Peel the mango and cut the pulp away from the pit, then cut the flesh into 1/2-inch dice. Peel the papayas, cut them in half lengthwise and spoon out the seeds, then cut lengthwise into thin wedges.

2. Twist the stem off the pineapple and stand it on end. Remove the peel by cutting down around the sides, deep enough to cut under the little pits. Cut it lengthwise in quarters and then trim away the strip of core that runs along each of the wedges. Cut each of these quarters in half lengthwise. Slice the strips crosswise into 1/4-inch-thick wedges.

3. Sprinkle the onion slices with the coarse salt and rub them between your hands until you no longer feel the salt. Drain in a colander for 15 minutes. Wring out as much liquid as you can by squeezing small bunches of the slices in your fists. Within an hour of serving, peel the avocados and cut them lengthwise into wedges.

4. Just before serving, gently toss together the fruit, onions, avocado, bell peppers, chiles, and cilantro with the olive oil and vinegar. Season to taste with salt and freshly ground pepper. Chill in the refrigerator while you're grilling the shrimp. (The salad should be cool but not cold.)

5. Grill the shrimp as shown on page 161 and immediately toss into the salad. Give the salad one final toss and serve, making sure everyone has his or her fair share of shrimp. Season with freshly ground pepper and garnish each serving with a sprig of mint, if desired.

1 ripe mango (about 1 pound)

2 ripe Hawaiian papayas or 1 Mexican papaya (about 3 pounds total)

1 pineapple

1 medium red onion, sliced thin

2 teaspoons coarse salt

2 ripe avocados, preferably Hass

1 red bell pepper, charred, peeled (see page 20), stemmed, seeded, and cut into 1/4-inch-wide strips

1 yellow bell pepper, charred, peeled (see page 20), stemmed, seeded, and cut into 1/4-inch-wide strips

2 poblano chiles, peeled, stemmed, seeded, and cut into 1/4-inch-wide strips

2 jalapeño chiles, seeded and chopped fine

leaves and small stems from one small bunch cilantro, chopped fine

2/3 cup extra virgin olive oil

1/3 cup sherry wine vinegar

pepper to taste

30 large or 20 jumbo shrimp for first courses, 30 large or 18 jumbo shrimp for main courses

mint sprigs for garnish (optional)

Celery Root and Shrimp Salad

MAKES: 8 first course servings

1 medium celeriac

1 tablespoon fresh lemon juice

1 cup mayonnaise, preferably homemade
(see Basic Mayonnaise, page 176)

¼ cup extra virgin olive oil, if you're using
bottled mayonnaise

1 tablespoon Dijon mustard

1 medium bunch parsley, preferably
Italian flat leaf, large stems removed,
chopped very fine

1 medium bunch chives, chopped very
fine (optional)

24 large shrimp

salt and pepper to taste

*This salad derives from the French classic céleriac rémoulade, in which thin strips of celeriac (also called celery root) are tossed with a mayonnaise with plenty of mustard in it. If you're not familiar with celeriac, it's a large and bulbous root with little growths coming out of it—not appetizing-looking at all, but with the flavor of celery made subtle and exotic and with a texture all its own. When shopping for celeriac, lift it to sense its weight; it should be heavy and dense, not light and spongy.
To make this salad you can keep things simple and use bottled mayonnaise—I like to work a little extra virgin olive oil into bottled mayonnaise to make it taste homemade—but it's not much harder to make your own, and the salad tastes so much better. You can further fool around with the flavor of the mayonnaise by adding such goodies as reduced mushroom cooking liquid, mussel cooking liquid, or shrimp broth; by trying different vinegars and oils (a small amount of hazelnut oil added to a basic mayonnaise also works miracles); or by adding different herbs, such as chopped chives or tarragon. For special occasions, a little shaved truffle wouldn't hurt either. But, simple or complex, what gives this salad its charm is the delightful interplay of textures.*

1. Peel the celeriac with a sharp paring knife and slice it into rounds about the thickness of two quarters using a knife or a Japanese plastic vegetable slicer (or mandoline). Cut the rounds into julienne strips as wide as they are thick and toss with the lemon juice. If you're using bottled mayonnaise, whisk the olive oil into it in a small bowl. Add the mustard to whichever mayonnaise you're using and spoon the mayonnaise over the celeriac. Add the parsley and chives to the celeriac; toss with a couple of spoons.

2. Cook the shrimp by plunging them in about 3 quarts of boiling water and boiling for 2 minutes. Drain in a colander, rinse with cold water, peel, devein, and cut each shrimp into 3 pieces lengthwise. Add to the celeriac and toss. Season the mixture to taste with salt and pepper.

8 ounces *haricots verts* or American green beans

salt

1 pound white or green asparagus

18 large shrimp for first courses or 16 jumbo shrimp for main courses

¼ cup sherry vinegar

¾ cup heavy cream or crème fraîche

pepper to taste

1 small bunch chervil or the green fronds from a fennel bulb, chopped, 10 or 6 sprigs reserved for garnish (optional)

4 ounces terrine of foie gras, chilled and cut into ½-inch dice (optional)

10 ounces cultivated mushrooms or assorted wild mushrooms

Mushroom, *Haricot Vert,* Asparagus, and Shrimp Salad

MAKES: 10 first course or 6 main course servings

This elegant salad uses a whole interplay of textures to emphasize the gentle crunch of the shrimp. Use white asparagus if you can find it—it's striking alongside the green beans—and feel free to augment the flavors with fresh herbs, such as tarragon or chives. The dressing is very simple— cream thickened with a little vinegar—and while it's rich, you don't need much. As an ultimate luxury, include diced terrine of foie gras. If you can't find the thin French-style string beans called haricots verts, *buy regular string beans and "French" them by cutting them in half lengthwise and then each half in half again. Be sure to buy the best-quality shrimp you can for this—wild Gulf shrimp, if possible—so its flavor shines through. If you have a big spider utensil or skimmer, you can use the same water to cook everything and just fish out each item as you go along. (A spider looks like a spider web with a long handle attached and is usually used for deep-frying.)*

1. Snap off both ends of the *haricots verts* and plunge them in about 4 quarts of salted boiling water until they retain only the tiniest bit of crunch, about 4 minutes. (French the beans if you're using American-style beans; see note above.) Drain in a colander and rinse under cold water. Chill in the refrigerator.

2. Cut off 2 inches from the base of the asparagus spears and discard. Use a vegetable peeler to peel the spears from the base of the flower all the way to the bottom. Cook the asparagus in about 4 quarts of rapidly boiling salted water until the spears retain only the slightest crunch, about 4 minutes. Drain in a colander and rinse immediately with cold water. Cut each spear into 3 sections. Refrigerate until needed.

3. Cook the shrimp by plunging them in about 3 quarts of boiling water and boiling for 2 minutes for large shrimp and 3 minutes for jumbo shrimp. Drain in a colander and rinse with cold water. Peel the shrimp and, if you wish, devein them. Set aside.

4. Pour the vinegar in a small saucepan and boil down by half. Let cool to room temperature and, in a small mixing bowl, combine it with the cream and add salt and pepper to taste. Stir the chopped chervil into the dressing.

5. Within 30 minutes of serving, slice the mushrooms between 1/8- and 1/4-inch thick and place them in a mixing bowl large enough to hold all the salad. If you're using wild mushrooms, slice them along their contours with a small knife so you can see their shapes. Add the reserved ingredients and drizzle with the dressing. Toss gently with two spoons and arrange in a mound on chilled plates. Garnish each serving with a sprig of chervil, if desired.

30 | simply shrimp

Tomato and Shrimp Salad

MAKES: 8 first course servings

If you can't find tomatoes at their prime, use cherry tomatoes or even the new "grape" tomatoes that have begun to appear in grocery stores. If you're a fanatic, you can peel these small tomatoes by plunging them in boiling water for about 15 seconds and then rinsing them immediately under cold water. You then carefully pull away the peel with a paring knife; all of this is best done the night before while watching television. I almost always peel regular tomatoes, using the same process, but this too is optional—especially when tomatoes are at their height and so full of flavor than no one notices a peel. Dress this salad at the last minute—if you add salt any sooner it will draw water out of the tomatoes and make the oil-and-vinegar dressing watery. You can add herbs—tarragon and marjoram are especially good, but not the two together—but the better the tomatoes, the less need to elaborate. Use your best olive oil.

2 pints cherry or grape tomatoes or 2 pounds regular tomatoes

24 large shrimp

1 tablespoon fresh tarragon leaves or 2 teaspoons fresh marjoram leaves, chopped just before adding to the salad (optional)

¼ cup extra virgin olive oil

2 tablespoons excellent vinegar, such as balsamic, sherry, or homemade

salt and pepper to taste

parsley or chervil sprigs for garnish (optional)

1. Peel the regular tomatoes (page 21) or the cherry or grape tomatoes, if desired. Cut regular tomatoes into wedges about ¾-inch wide on the outside. The exact number of wedges per tomato depends on the size of the tomatoes—usually you'll have between 6 and 12. As an additional refinement, you can remove the seeds by sliding your finger along the side of each of the wedges and pushing the seeds out. If you're using cherry or grape tomatoes, cut them in half through the side.

2. Cook the shrimp by plunging them in about 3 quarts of boiling water and boiling for 2 minutes. Drain in a colander and rinse with cold water. Peel the shrimp and, if you wish, devein them.

3. Just before serving, combine the shrimp with the tomatoes, sprinkle with the herbs if you're using them, add the oil and vinegar, and season to taste with salt and pepper. Decorate each serving with a sprig of parsley or chervil, if desired.

TOMATO AND SHRIMP SALAD VARIATIONS: The combination of tomatoes and shrimp can be used as a jumping off point for any number of variations. Bell peppers, charred, peeled, and cut into strips or sections and combined with French string beans are an especially beautiful combination (see photo, above), as are artichoke bottoms and frisée combined with *haricots verts* (see photo, opposite).

Cold Shrimp Salad with Capers and Dill

MAKES: 8 first course servings

40 large or 30 jumbo shrimp, peeled and deveined (deveining optional)

2 tablespoons olive oil

2 cloves garlic, minced and crushed to a paste with the side of a chef's knife

½ medium red onion, sliced as thinly as possible

2 teaspoons coarse salt

½ cup mayonnaise, preferably homemade (see variations on pages 176–79)

2 tablespoons capers, drained

3 tablespoons fresh lemon juice

2 tablespoons fresh dill, minced

1 small bunch parsley, large stems removed, leaves and small stems chopped fine

1 dried chipotle chile, soaked for 30 minutes in warm water and drained, or 1 canned chipotle chile in adobo sauce, sauce rinsed off, or 1 jalapeño chile; stemmed, seeded, and chopped very fine

salt and pepper to taste

This zesty salad is inspired by a mussel salad—apparently popular in Nantucket—that appeared in Saveur *magazine. It just so happens that the same ingredients are great with shrimp.*

1. Sauté the shrimp over high heat in the olive oil for about 3 minutes for large, 4 minutes for jumbo. Turn the heat down to low and add the garlic. Toss or stir the shrimp with the garlic for about 30 seconds, until the garlic aroma fills the room but not enough to let it burn. Set aside and let cool, then refrigerate for at least an hour.

2. Sprinkle the onion slices with the coarse salt and rub them between your hands until you no longer feel the salt. Drain in a colander for 15 minutes. Wring out as much liquid as you can by squeezing small bunches of the slices in your fists.

3. Combine the mayonnaise, capers, lemon juice, dill, and parsley in a salad bowl. Add the shrimp, onion slices, and chile, and toss. Season to taste with salt and pepper, and serve.

Indian Salad with Potatoes and Shrimp

MAKES: 6 first course or side dish servings

This recipe derives from the Indian dish chat, *a kind of potato salad considered somewhat of a poor man's dish but somehow immensely satisfying with its juxtaposition of herbs, saltiness, and tartness. The tartness is typically contributed by dried mango powder, but lime juice will also work. You can use the same flavor combinations and spices with other ingredients added to the salad, such as cucumbers, mushrooms, or tomatoes.*

1. Sauté the shrimp in the oil for about 3 minutes over medium to high heat and let cool. Refrigerate for at least an hour. Reserve the oil in the pan.

2. Put the potatoes in a small pot with enough cold water to cover and bring them to a gentle simmer. Cook until you can pierce them with a knife but stop before they're completely soft, 20 to 25 minutes. Drain, let cool slightly, and peel. Slice into 1/3-inch-thick slices and spread on a sheet pan or a sheet of wax paper—don't heap up the potatoes or they'll stick together.

3. Sprinkle the onion slices with the coarse salt and rub them between your hands until you no longer feel the salt. Drain in a colander for 15 minutes. Wring out as much liquid as you can by squeezing small bunches of the slices in your fists.

4. Put the cumin and coriander into the pan that you used to sauté the shrimp and place over low heat. Cook, stirring, for about 2 minutes or until the spices are fragrant, remove from the heat, and allow to cool. Add the cayenne, black pepper, and lime juice to the pan and then add the shrimp. Stir the shrimp around until it is well coated with the spice mixture.

5. Sprinkle the potatoes with the chopped cilantro and mint and salt to taste. In a salad bowl or on individual plates, layer the potatoes and shrimp and any sauce left in the pan.

30 large shrimp, peeled and deveined (deveining optional)

2 tablespoons olive oil or vegetable oil

3 medium to large white waxy potatoes (1 ½ pounds)

1 medium red onion, sliced as thinly as possible

2 teaspoons coarse salt

3 tablespoons ground cumin

4 tablespoons ground coriander

1 tablespoon cayenne pepper

2 teaspoons freshly ground black pepper

3 tablespoons fresh lime juice

1 small bunch cilantro, large stems removed, leaves and small stems chopped fine

1 small bunch mint, large stems removed, leaves and small stems chopped fine

fine salt to taste

Classic Shrimp Cocktail

MAKES: 6 first course servings

There are a few American classics that seem never to disappoint and can be reliable standbys, especially in an uncertain place or restaurant. This should not sound equivocal, since shrimp cocktail, made in the usual way, is perfectly wonderful. In Europe cold shrimp are always served with the heads on, while in the United States they're usually decapitated. The choice is yours. Cook the shrimp in their shells and peel them afterward so they retain more flavor.

1. Cook the shrimp by plunging them in about 3 quarts of boiling water and boiling for 2 minutes. Drain in a colander and rinse with cold water. Peel the shrimp and, if you wish, devein them. Refrigerate for at least an hour or until well chilled.

2. Combine the ketchup, chili sauce, horseradish, Tabasco, and lemon juice in a mixing bowl. Serve the sauce in small ramekins or cocktail glasses. Arrange the shrimp on the rim of cocktail stem glasses, if desired. Garnish with a lemon wedge.

30 large shrimp

⅔ cup ketchup

⅔ cup chili sauce

¼ cup grated horseradish from a jar, or about 2 inches fresh horseradish root, grated

1 ½ teaspoons Tabasco sauce, or more to taste

3 teaspoons fresh lemon juice, or more to taste

1 lemon, cut into 6 wedges

Truffle and Shrimp Salad

MAKES: 4 first course servings

This luxurious salad is worthy of your most elegant dinners. Use the best shrimp you can find—ideally wild Gulf shrimp.

¼ cup heavy cream

1 egg yolk

1 black truffle, as large as you dare and can afford

12 jumbo shrimp (preferably wild Gulf white shrimp)

2 tablespoons excellent quality sherry vinegar or balsamic vinegar

¼ cup walnut oil (preferably made from roasted nuts) or excellent quality extra virgin olive oil

salt and pepper to taste

4 sprigs chervil (optional)

1. Whisk together the cream and egg yolk in a small bowl.

2. Slice the truffle as thinly as you can with a truffle slicer or a plastic Japanese mandoline (the best brand is Benriner) and combine the slices with the cream and egg mixture. Cover the bowl with plastic wrap, making sure it touches the surface of the mixture, and refrigerate overnight.

3. Cook the shrimp by plunging them in about 2 quarts of boiling water and boiling for 4 minutes. Drain in a colander and rinse with cold water. Let cool and refrigerate for at least an hour.

4. Use a slotted spoon to take the truffle slices out of the egg yolk mixture and reserve. Whisk in the vinegar. Gently whisk in the oil, a teaspoon at a time. If you're using olive oil, use a wooden spoon and don't beat the mixture or the oil will turn bitter. Season to taste with salt and pepper.

5. Peel and devein the shrimp and toss with the sauce and reserved truffle slices. Place 3 shrimp on each plate and garnish each with a sprig of chervil, if desired.

Shrimp and Truffles

Some of us justify eating truffles at home by imagining how much money we're saving by not going out. True, their price is horrendous, but when the cost of a well-truffled dinner at home is compared with a truffleless meal in a fine French restaurant, well, the logic is apparent. It's like the thousands you save each day by walking past the bejeweled window of Harry Winston and not going in.

There are, of course, truffles and then there are truffles, and the range in quality is disturbing, since there's so much at stake. In addition to knowing about the various kinds and how they're sold, it's imperative that you be sure that they are fresh or, if frozen, that they were frozen immediately after coming out of the earth. Your best bet for ensuring either of these conditions is a trustworthy supplier and to organize your special dinner around the day of the truffles' arrival in the United States.

You're likely to run into three kinds of truffles: black winter truffles, which come from France, Italy, and China (the best ones are usually the French ones); white winter truffles, which come from Northern Italy; and black summer truffles, which come from Italy (mainly Tuscany). White truffles are the most expensive and are shaved raw over innumerable dishes, but most commonly pasta. Black winter truffles are almost always cooked and end up in all manner of braised and stewed dishes, even though long cooking tends to dissipate their flavor. Black summer truffles have less flavor than black winter truffles but are also far less expensive so you can use more. When they're fresh, they're a bargain.

Black truffles come fresh, frozen, bottled, and canned. The canned versions are not worth bothering with; good quality bottled versions will give you some truffle flavor and effect but they won't have that permeating nature of fresh and properly frozen truffles. Frozen truffles are often the best option since they can be frozen faster than they can be shipped, but their texture may be compromised. This point may become less important if they're being cooked.

The trick to getting the most out of truffles is to give them time to permeate the dish in which they're being used. Another secret is that truffles have an affinity for fats—their aroma is trapped by the fat in butter, eggs, and cream—so by simply storing your truffles overnight with these items in a tightly sealed jar in the refrigerator, you can create your own sort of truffle seasoning.

When composing a shrimp dish with truffles, make sure your sauce has a fat (preferably emulsified fat) such as egg yolk (mayonnaise) or cream. If you're making a salad, use an emulsified sauce, such as a thin mayonnaise, rather than oil alone, which would give the truffle flavor a kind of one-dimensional quality.

Thai Shrimp and Cucumber Salad

MAKES: 6 first course servings

This is one of those dishes that's so characteristically Thai that you'd never mistake it as coming from another place. The combination of mint, cilantro, and, if you can find it, licorice-like holy basil combined with peanuts and coconut milk is easily addictive. Chop the cilantro, mint, and basil for this salad as close to serving as possible—the mint and basil lose their punch especially quickly once chopped.

30 large or 24 jumbo shrimp

2 tablespoons vegetable oil, such as canola oil

2 long hothouse cucumbers or 4 regular cucumbers, peeled

1 ½ teaspoons coarse salt

2 Thai or 4 jalapeño chiles, stemmed, seeded, and minced

1 clove garlic, minced and crushed to a paste with the side of a chef's knife

½ cup unsweetened coconut milk

1 tablespoon plus 1 ½ teaspoons sugar

¼ cup smooth natural peanut butter (should contain only peanuts and salt)

1 medium bunch cilantro, large stems removed, leaves and small stems chopped fine, 6 sprigs reserved for garniture (garniture optional)

about 20 basil leaves, preferably holy basil, chopped fine

3 tablespoons fresh lime juice

2 tablespoons rice wine vinegar or white wine vinegar

3 tablespoons Thai fish sauce, or more as needed

1. Sauté the shrimp over high heat in the oil, about 3 minutes for large and 4 minutes for jumbo. Allow to cool, then refrigerate for at least 1 hour.

2. Halve the cucumbers lengthwise and use a spoon to scoop the seeds out of each half. Slice the halves into crescents about ⅛-inch thick. Combine the cucumber slices with the coarse salt, rub with your hands until you no longer feel the salt, then drain in a colander for 15 minutes. Wring out as much liquid as you can by squeezing small bunches of the slices in your fists.

3. Add the chiles, garlic, 1 tablespoon of the coconut milk, and sugar to the peanut butter in a mixing bowl large enough to hold all the shrimp. Work the mixture with a whisk until smooth and add another 2 tablespoons of coconut milk. Work again until smooth, add the rest of the coconut milk, and work until smooth. Stir in the rest of the ingredients, except the mint or cilantro sprigs, and add the shrimp. Toss the shrimp until it's completely coated with the sauce, then add the cucumbers. Toss to coat the cucumbers, chill for at least an hour, and serve on chilled plates. Garnish each serving with a sprig of mint or cilantro, if desired.

Shrimp Escabèche

MAKES: 6 first course servings

1 small bunch cilantro (1 cup loose leaves), large stems removed

1 small bunch parsley, large stems removed

2/3 cup olive oil

1/3 cup excellent white or red wine vinegar or fresh lemon juice

1 clove garlic, minced and crushed to a paste with the side of a chef's knife

1 small red onion, sliced as thinly as possible

1/2 teaspoon ground cumin

1/2 teaspoon ground coriander

1/4 cup golden raisins (sultanas)

1/2 teaspoon saffron threads, soaked for 30 minutes in 1 tablespoon water

1 cup dark olives, pitted

2 heaping tablespoons diced preserved lemons (optional; these are available in most gourmet grocery stores)

30 large shrimp, boiled, peeled, and deveined (deveining optional)

seeds from half a pomegranate (optional)

Every country in the Mediterranean has some version of escabèche, *which can be defined as seafood, often with vegetables, that's marinated after it's been cooked instead of, or in addition to, being marinated first. This cooking method may have come about as a way of preserving fish, since once fish is cooked and especially when it's surrounded with an acidic mixture, it stays fresh for several days. Certain ingredients are almost universal—vinegar, olive oil, and herbs—but once you understand the idea,* escabèches *can be flavored with just about anything that tastes good. Raisins, nuts, and olives suggest a Middle Eastern interpretation; saffron and preserved lemons suggest Morocco; cilantro and chiles evoke Mexico (the Gulf is their Mediterranean); and fino sherry conjures up the Catalan region of Spain. The version given here leans toward Morocco. Whatever you come up with, use your best vinegar and olive oil, but don't use extra virgin olive oil for the herb mixture, or the blender will make it bitter. Keep this recipe in mind if you have leftover grilled shrimp.*

1. Combine the cilantro, parsley, 1/4 cup olive oil, vinegar, and garlic in a blender and purée for 1 minute.

2. Cook the onion slices in 2 tablespoons of olive oil in a small pan over medium heat until they turn translucent, about 8 minutes. Add the spices and cook over medium heat until fragrant, about 1 minute. Combine the onion mixture with the herb mixture. Add the remaining olive oil, the raisins, the saffron and its soaking liquid, the olives, and the preserved lemons, if using, in a dish just large enough to hold the shrimp in a single layer. Thoroughly combine the shrimp with the mixture, sprinkle with the pomegranate seeds (if using), cover, and refrigerate for 12 hours and up to 3 days.

Grilled Bell Pepper, Basil, Anchovy, and Shrimp Salad

MAKES: 4 generous first course servings

You can spice up this colorful salad by including a poblano chile or two, but if you don't like the heat just leave it out. Substitute cherry or "grape" tomatoes if you can't find large tomatoes. The bread in this salad, which is inspired by the Tuscan panzanella, *adds a contrasting crunch and absorbs some of the juices; add it just before serving so it doesn't get soggy.*

1. Place the peppers and chiles in a large salad bowl. Soak the anchovies in water for 5 minutes to remove some of their saltiness and add them to the peppers and chiles.

2. Cook the shrimp by plunging them in about 3 quarts of boiling water and boiling for 2 minutes. Drain in a colander and rinse with cold water. Peel the shrimp and, if you wish, devein them. Refrigerate at least an hour.

3. Bake the bread cubes in a 300°F oven for 10 to 15 minutes until they're lightly toasted and crunchy. Add the tomatoes and basil leaves to the salad.

4. Just before serving, sprinkle the bread cubes over the salad and add the oil, vinegar, and shrimp, and toss. Season to taste with salt and pepper, keeping in mind that the anchovies may still be very salty.

2 bell peppers, preferably one red and one yellow, charred, peeled (see page 20), seeded, cut into ¾-inch strips and diced

2 poblano chiles, charred, peeled (see page 20), seeded, cut into ¾-inch strips, and diced

24 bottled anchovies, or more or less to taste

20 large shrimp

3 slices crusty French bread from a boule or the equivalent from a baguette, cut into ½-inch cubes

4 medium tomatoes, peeled, stemmed, seeded (see page 21), and each sliced into 6 wedges

1 bunch basil, stems removed

¼ cup extra virgin olive oil

3 tablespoons good quality red wine vinegar or balsamic vinegar, or 6 tablespoons inexpensive balsamic vinegar boiled down to 3 tablespoons

salt and pepper to taste

Japanese Shrimp and Cucumber Salad

MAKES: 8 hors d'oeuvre servings (2 shrimp per person)

This is a great little hors d'oeuvre, best served with chopsticks, for people to reach for while sitting around having cocktails. If you like, you can serve various Japanese pickled vegetables as well as the cucumbers, but the cucumbers are more refreshing and less overbearingly salty than most pickled foods.

1. Cook the shrimp by plunging them in about 2 quarts of boiling water and boiling for 3 minutes for extra large shrimp and 4 minutes for jumbo. Drain in a colander and rinse with cold water. Peel the shrimp and, if you wish, devein them. Chill in the refrigerator for at least an hour.

2. Halve the cucumbers lengthwise and use a spoon to scoop the seeds out of each half. Slice the halves into crescents about 1/8-inch thick. Combine the cucumber slices with the coarse salt, rub with your hands until you no longer feel the salt, then drain in a colander for 15 minutes. Wring out as much liquid as you can by squeezing small bunches of the slices in your fists.

3. If you're not using the bonito flakes, combine the vinegar, soy sauce, water, and sugar in a small bowl and set aside. If you are using the bonito flakes, combine the ingredients in a saucepan and bring to a boil. As soon as the mixture reaches a boil, turn off the heat and add the bonito flakes. Let steep for 5 minutes, then strain. Discard the used bonito flakes and chill the sauce.

4. Just before serving, add the scallions to the sauce. Serve the shrimp next to the cucumbers, with the sauce in a separate dish for dipping.

16 extra large or jumbo shrimp

1 hothouse cucumber or 2 regular cucumbers, peeled

2 teaspoons coarse salt

1/4 cup rice wine vinegar

2 tablespoons Japanese soy sauce

1/4 cup water

1 tablespoon sugar

1/2 cup loosely packed bonito flakes (optional)

1 scallion, white part and 3 inches of the green, sliced very fine

Tabbouleh with Shrimp

MAKES: 4 to 6 side dish servings

Most of the tabbouleh one encounters in Near Eastern restaurants is a rather insipid mixture of bulghur—hulled, steamed, dried, and ground wheat—with a lot of lemon juice and indifferent olive oil. Paula Wolfert, who has written several wonderful books about Mediterranean cooking, provides some insight into how it ought to taste: The word is derived from tabil, which is Arabic for "spice." The other secret is a pile of freshly chopped herbs—they must be chopped by hand, so arm yourself with your biggest and sharpest knife—and the best olive oil; fruity, grassy, green oil seems to work best.

¾ cup fine-grain bulghur

1 small bunch chives (about 30 sprigs)

1 large bunch parsley, preferably Italian flat leaf, stems removed

2 bunches mint, stems removed

6 tablespoons extra virgin olive oil

30 medium shrimp

1 cucumber, peeled

1 ½ teaspoons coarse salt

½ teaspoon cayenne

¼ teaspoon allspice

¼ teaspoon cinnamon

⅛ teaspoon cloves

⅛ teaspoon nutmeg

¼ cup fresh lemon juice

4 medium tomatoes, peeled, stemmed, seeded (see page 21), chopped medium fine, tossed with ½ teaspoon salt, and drained in a fine-mesh strainer for 30 minutes

salt and pepper to taste

1. Rinse the bulghur in a fine-mesh strainer and put it in a bowl. Pour in 1 ½ cups of boiling water and let sit for 30 minutes. Turn out onto a clean kitchen towel and squeeze out the excess liquid. Sprinkle the herbs with about a tablespoon of the olive oil—this seals in the flavor and keeps the mint from blackening—and chop fine by hand. Toss the herbs and the rest of the olive oil with the bulghur in a large bowl.

2. Cook the shrimp by plunging them in 3 quarts of boiling water and boiling for 2 minutes. Drain in a colander and rinse with cold water. Peel the shrimp and, if you wish, devein them.

3. Halve the cucumber lengthwise and use a spoon to scoop the seeds out of each half. Cut the halves lengthwise into strips and cut these strips in half lengthwise so each strip is about ¼-inch wide. Slice the strips crosswise to make ¼-inch dice. Combine the cucumber cubes with the coarse salt and rub them together until you no longer feel the salt. Let drain in a colander for 30 minutes. Wring out as much liquid as you can by squeezing small bunches of the cubes in your fists.

4. In a medium bowl, gently stir together the cucumbers, spices, lemon juice, and tomatoes, and then stir this mixture into the bulghur. Stir in the shrimp. Season to taste with salt and pepper. Cover and refrigerate overnight.

Shrimp with Tropical Fruit Salsa and *Sauce Crevettes*

MAKES: 8 first course servings

The trick to this elegant little first course is the juxtaposition of a rich traditional sauce with a modern salsa. The sweet and sour tang of the salsa lightens the whole effect while the shrimp cream sauce—called Sauce Crevettes—gives the dish a deep, complex flavor. The amounts given here make more sauce than you'll need, but you can freeze the rest and use it for future shrimp dishes—it's great stirred into shrimp soup or stew dishes to reinforce the shrimp flavor. If the sauce appears to have separated once thawed, bring 1/4 cup heavy cream to a gentle simmer and simmer about 2 minutes. Over low to medium heat, whisk in the separated sauce and it will re-emulsify.

1. Heat the *Sauce Crevettes*—boil it for a minute or two if you want it thicker—and spoon about 3 tablespoons in the center of 8 small heated plates. Place a shrimp on top and a dollop of the salsa on top of the shrimp. Serve immediately.

8 jumbo shrimp, sautéed in olive oil for 4 minutes, peeled, and deveined

1 ½ cups *Sauce Crevettes* (see page 173)

1 cup Tropical Fruit Salsa (about ⅕ recipe; see page 172)

Jumbo Shrimp with Caviar

MAKES: 6 first course servings

This recipe is unabashedly extravagant, but it is also a good way to serve caviar and experience its luxury without having to serve a large amount.

Cook the shrimp by plunging them in about 2 quarts of boiling water and boiling for 4 minutes. Drain in a colander and rinse with cold water. Peel the shrimp and, if you wish, devein them. Chill in the refrigerator for about an hour. If you're using the sauce, place a tablespoon in a round in the center of 6 chilled plates. Place a shrimp on top and mound each shrimp with a tablespoon of caviar.

VARIATION: Sea urchin roe, now popular in sushi bars, isn't cheap but it's a lot less expensive than caviar. Try topping your shrimp with a table-spoon of this roe instead of the caviar. Alternatively, you can use salmon roe, which is also sold at sushi bars in small amounts.

6 jumbo shrimp

3 ounces caviar

Aigrelette Sauce (recipe follows)

Aigrelette Sauce

MAKES: 6 tablespoons (for 1 recipe of Jumbo Shrimp with Caviar)

This tangy green sauce is a nice counterpoint to the richness of the caviar and shrimp. The green color is for effect only and isn't essential, but it looks very pretty on the plate.

In a small mixing bowl, combine the egg yolk with the mustard. Work in the oil ½ teaspoon at a time. Stir in the rest of the ingredients.

1 egg yolk

1 teaspoon, or more to taste, Dijon mustard, preferably Maille brand fines herbes (which is green)

3 tablespoons hazelnut oil made from roasted nuts (LeBlanc is a good brand)

1 teaspoon chlorophyll (see page 182; optional)

2 teaspoons good quality white wine vinegar, such as champagne vinegar or sherry vinegar, or more to taste

2 teaspoons truffle juice, or more to taste (optional)

salt to taste (note that caviar is usually quite salty)

Shrimp and Bacon
Hors d'Oeuvres

MAKES: 8 hors d'oeuvre servings (16 shrimp)

¾ pound bacon, sliced thin (16 slices)

1 dried chipotle chile, soaked for 30 minutes in warm water and drained, or 1 canned chipotle chile in adobo sauce, or 1 jalapeño chile; stemmed, seeded, and chopped very fine

16 large shrimp, preferably wild Gulf shrimp, peeled and deveined

Long an American cliché, these little hors d'oeuvres are so delicious with cocktails that we all need to be reminded of them. The trick is to use wild Gulf shrimp or, if you're using farmed shrimp, to brine them as described on page 15. The crunch is important.

A second factor essential to success is that the bacon be sliced very thin so that it cooks and gets crispy before you overcook the shrimp. This can be a problem if you have access only to presliced bacon, but the recipe is still worth doing. If you can find slab bacon, chill it in the freezer until it's very firm and then slice it as thinly as you can. The other trick is to precook the bacon slightly to get it started. If you like a little heat, be sure to include the chile.

1. Preheat the oven to 350°F. Place the bacon slices on a plate in the microwave for 1 to 1 ½ minutes on high until the bacon renders most of its fat but is still pliable. The goal is to cook the bacon as much as possible without making it brittle.

2. Place a pinch of chopped chile on each bacon slice. Wrap a bacon slice around the center of each shrimp and hold the bacon in place with a toothpick. Bake for 12 to 15 minutes. Serve immediately.

Shrimp-stuffed Hard-boiled Eggs

MAKES: 12 egg halves

By experimenting with different sauces (especially the mayonnaises on pages 176–79) and additional flavorings such as peppers, chiles, mushrooms, tomatoes, and even fruit, you'll ensure that your deviled eggs will never again be boring. Deviled eggs are also a good use for leftover cooked shrimp, which can be frozen until you need it, because the sauce counteracts any dryness in the shrimp.

1. Use a thumbtack or pin to make a tiny hole in the rounder end of each egg. (This allows air in the eggs to escape as it expands and keeps the shells from cracking and marking the whites.) Place the eggs in a pot with enough cold water to cover and turn the heat on high. As soon as the water comes to a simmer, turn down the heat to maintain a simmer (not a hard boil) and start timing. Cook the eggs, from the time the water came to a simmer, for 10 minutes, and drain—don't overcook. Rinse with cold water and let sit in a bowl of cold water until cool. To make the shells easier to remove, tap the eggs to crack them and soak for 10 minutes more before peeling.

2. Combine the shrimp with one of the mayonnaises.

3. Peel the eggs and slice them in half lengthwise. Gently spoon out the yolks—when properly cooked they should still look shiny, bright yellow, and moist—and combine the yolks with the shrimp mixture. Season the mixture to taste with salt and pepper. Fill the eggs with the mixture, mounding it in the hollow left by the yolk.

6 extra large eggs

12 large cooked shrimp, peeled, deveined, and chopped into a ½-inch dice

3 tablespoons Curry Mayonnaise (page 179), Saffron Aioli (page 179), or Caper and Herb Mayonnaise (page 178)

salt and pepper to taste

Thai Shrimp "Bruschetta"

MAKES: 24 *bruschette*

The most famous bruschette—*the plural, pronounced* broo-SKE-tay—*are the little chicken liver canapés served in restaurants in Tuscany. Variations have become so common that nowadays just about anything served on a piece of baguette toast qualifies. You can make up your own variations using different relishes, salsas, and chutneys, but this one is particularly worth trying because of its Thai flavors and the sweet marinated cucumbers.*

1. Halve the cucumber lengthwise and use a spoon to scoop the seeds out of each half. Slice the cucumber lengthwise into ¼-inch-wide strips. Cut the strips crosswise to make ¼-inch dice. Toss the dice with the sugar and rub in your hands until you don't feel the sugar. Let drain in a colander for 30 minutes.

2. Combine the diced tomatoes with the chiles.

3. Squeeze the cucumber dice in your fists to extract as much liquid as possible. Toss the cucumber with the fish sauce.

4. Just before serving, place 1 ½ teaspoons cucumber dice on the baguette slices. Place 2 shrimp halves on the cucumber and top with a teaspoon of tomato dice. Place a mint leaf on each.

1 long hothouse cucumber, peeled

3 tablespoons sugar

2 dried chipotle chiles, soaked for 30 minutes in warm water and drained, or 2 canned chipotle chiles in adobo sauce, sauce rinsed off, or 2 jalapeño chiles; stemmed, seeded, and chopped fine

2 tomatoes, peeled, stemmed, seeded (see page 21), and cut into ¼-inch dice

2 tablespoons Thai fish sauce or more to taste

24 ¼-inch-thick baguette slices, toasted under the broiler on one side only

24 large shrimp, sautéed in oil for 3 minutes, peeled, deveined, and halved horizontally

24 mint leaves

soups

Shrimp Bourride

MAKES: 8 first course or 6 main course servings

6 cups fish broth, Fat-free Shrimp Broth (see page 68), or chicken broth

4 tomatoes, chopped coarse

2 pounds large shrimp, peeled and deveined (deveining optional)

Saffron Aioli (see page 179)

24 baguette slices, toasted under the broiler on one side

A bourride is a Provençal soup or stew, traditionally made with Mediterranean fish, that's thickened with aioli just before serving. In this recipe, you start with a broth—fish broth, chicken broth, or broth made from shrimp heads or shells—and poach the peeled shrimp in it at the last minute. Then, just before serving, whisk about one third of the soup into a bowl of aioli and return this mixture back to the pot. The richness and thickness of this soup can be varied by using different ratios of aioli to soup base.

Bring the broth to a simmer with the tomatoes and simmer for 15 minutes over medium heat. Strain the tomato pulp through a food mill or coarse strainer, discarding the seeds and peels. Add the shrimp and simmer for 1 minute. Put half the aioli into a large metal bowl and whisk in about 1/3 of the soup. Take the soup off the heat and pour the aioli-soup mixture back into the pot. Whisk to combine and place over very low heat. Stir for 2 minutes, then ladle into hot soup bowls and pass the toasts and extra aioli at the table.

Creamy Shrimp Soup with Fresh Herbs

MAKES: 8 first course servings

The idea for this soup comes from a Northern French or Belgian method for cooking eels in which the cooking broth is finished with cream and thickened with egg yolks. The cream can be kept to a minimum and the egg yolks left out entirely if you prefer—it's the abundance of fresh herbs, chopped just before serving, that makes this soup a revelation.

3 medium leeks, green parts removed (they can be used in the broth) and white parts cleaned and sliced thin

2 tablespoons butter

6 cups shrimp, fish, or chicken broth

1 small bouquet garni (see box, opposite)

1 medium bunch parsley, preferably Italian flat leaf, large stems removed

1 small bunch tarragon, stemmed

1 medium bunch mint, stemmed

1 bunch chives

1 medium bunch sorrel, stemmed (optional)

½ to 1 cup heavy cream

2 pounds large shrimp, peeled and deveined (deveining optional)

6 egg yolks (optional)

salt and pepper to taste

1. In a heavy pot large enough to hold the soup, cook the sliced leeks in the butter over low to medium heat, stirring regularly so they soften without browning, about 20 minutes. Add the broth and the bouquet garni and simmer for 15 minutes.

2. While the broth is simmering, chop the herbs very fine. Take the bouquet garni (and the green parts of the leeks, if using) out of the broth and add the herbs and cream. Bring to a simmer and add the shrimp. If you're not using the egg yolks, simmer for 2 minutes and serve; if you are, whisk the egg yolks with about 2 cups of the broth in a metal mixing bowl. Take the soup off the heat and whisk in the yolk mixture. Put over the very lowest possible heat and stir for 2 minutes with a wooden spoon, reaching into the corners so the eggs don't curdle there. As soon as the soup takes on a shiny, silky consistency, take it off the heat. Continue stirring for 5 minutes so the heat retained in the pot doesn't overcook the eggs. If you accidentally curdle the eggs, purée the soup with an immersion blender or regular blender. Season to taste with salt and pepper. Serve in hot bowls.

What Is a Bouquet Garni?

A bouquet garni is a little bundle of herbs—usually thyme, bay leaf, and parsley—tied together with some leek or scallion greens. If you have thyme on the stem instead of thyme leaves, just tie everything together with string. If you have dried thyme, wrap it in a little packet of cheesecloth. For 2 quarts of liquid include a small bunch of parsley, about 5 sprigs (or 1 teaspoon) of thyme, 1 imported bay leaf, and use the greens from 4 leeks or 7 scallions. Don't worry if you're missing one of the components.

Brazilian Coconut Peanut Shrimp Soup

MAKES: 8 first course or 6 main course servings

The idea for this soup comes from the Brazilian vatapa, *a hearty stew flavored with peanut butter and coconut milk and usually containing chicken. The formula is a great one with shrimp and the soup works especially well with chicken broth so you can save your precious shrimp broth for other culinary adventures. The optional chipotle chiles aren't traditional but they add a note of complex smokiness to the whole concoction.*

1. Over medium heat, cook the onion and garlic in the oil in a heavy-bottomed pot large enough to hold the soup. Stir regularly until the onion becomes shiny and translucent but doesn't brown, about 10 minutes. Add the broth and the tomatoes. Simmer for 15 minutes and strain the soup through a food mill or strainer, forcing the tomato pulp through and leaving behind the seeds and skins. Put the broth back in the pot and bring to a simmer.

2. In a small mixing bowl, work about a cup of the broth into the peanut butter, a little at a time, until the mixture is smooth and well combined. Add the peanut mixture to the broth along with the shrimp, coconut milk, chiles, if using, and lime juice. Simmer for 2 minutes and season to taste with salt and pepper. Serve in heated soup bowls. Swirl a teaspoon or so of shrimp butter on top of each serving, if desired.

1 large onion, chopped fine

3 cloves garlic, chopped fine

2 tablespoons olive oil or vegetable oil

6 cups chicken broth

4 medium tomatoes, chopped coarse

½ cup smooth natural peanut butter (should contain only peanuts and salt)

2 pounds large shrimp, peeled, deveined, and cut into ½-inch dice

1 cup unsweetened coconut milk

3 jalapeño chiles, or 3 chipotle chiles in adobo sauce, sauce rinsed off, or 3 dried chipotle chiles, soaked for 30 minutes in warm water and drained; stemmed, seeded, and chopped fine (optional)

5 tablespoons fresh lime juice

salt and pepper to taste

8 teaspoons Shrimp Butter (optional; see page 183)

Thai Hot and Spicy Shrimp Soup

MAKES: 6 first course servings

One of the great revelations of this soup is that once you've tracked down a few inexpensive ingredients, the soup can be put together in minutes and you don't need broth. The ingredients are so flavorful that the soup can be made with water.

6 cups water

2 small green or red Thai "bird" chiles or 4 jalapeño chiles

3 cloves garlic, chopped fine

2 shallots, minced

two ¼-inch-thick slices of galangal or fresh ginger

4 kaffir lime leaves, cut into fine shreds

1 stalk lemongrass, white soft part sliced very thin

1 pound large shrimp, peeled and deveined (deveining optional)

1 small bunch cilantro, large stems removed

¼ to ½ cup Thai fish sauce

juice of 3 limes

pepper to taste

Bring the water to a simmer and add the chiles, garlic, shallots, galangal, lime leaves, and lemongrass and simmer gently for 12 minutes. Add the shrimp, simmer for 1 minute, and add the cilantro, ¼ cup fish sauce, and lime juice. Simmer for 1 minute more. Season to taste with pepper. If the soup tastes like it needs salt, add fish sauce—it's very salty and will contribute flavor—until the salt level is right. Serve in heated soup bowls.

Corn and Shrimp Soup

MAKES: 6 first course servings

This soup combines two naturally symbiotic flavors: corn and poblano chiles. You can simply include the chiles as described here—charring them first helps bring out their flavor—or you can convert them into a Poblano Cream Sauce that's swirled over the soup in each bowl (see variation below).

1 white or yellow onion, chopped fine

2 cloves garlic, minced

2 tablespoons olive oil

3 ears fresh corn, shucked and kernels removed with a paring knife

4 tomatoes

1 quart chicken broth or shrimp broth

2 jalapeño chiles, or 2 chipotle chiles in adobo sauce, sauce rinsed off, or 2 dried chipotle chiles, soaked for 30 minutes in warm water and drained, stemmed, seeded, and chopped fine

2 fresh poblano chiles, charred, peeled, stemmed, seeded (see page 20), and chopped

1 medium bunch cilantro, large stems removed

1 pound medium to large shrimp, peeled and deveined (deveining optional)

3 tablespoons fresh lime juice

1 cup heavy cream (optional)

salt and pepper to taste

1. Over medium heat, cook the onion and garlic in the oil in a heavy-bottomed pot large enough to hold the soup, until the onion turns shiny and translucent but doesn't brown, about 10 minutes.

2. If you want the soup perfectly smooth, you'll need to strain it, so there's no point in peeling the tomatoes. If you'd like the soup to have some texture, peel and seed the tomatoes (see page 21). In either case, chop them—coarse if you're straining, fine if you're not.

3. Add the corn, tomatoes, broth, and chiles—don't include the poblano chiles if you're making the Poblano Cream Sauce—to the onion mixture and turn the heat to high. Stir while scraping against the bottom of the pot with a wooden spoon so the corn doesn't burn. Reduce the heat to medium and simmer for about 20 minutes from the time the broth first comes to a simmer. Chop the cilantro—coarse if you're straining, fine if you're not—and add it to the soup. Purée the soup in a blender for about a minute. If you want your soup perfectly smooth and creamy, work it through a food mill or a coarse strainer and return it to the pot.

4. Bring the soup back to a simmer and add the shrimp, lime juice, and heavy cream. Simmer for 2 minutes more. Season to taste with salt and pepper, and ladle into warm soup bowls.

POBLANO CREAM SAUCE: Combine the roasted and chopped poblano chiles with 1/2 cup heavy cream—use the remaining 1/2 cup cream for the rest of the recipe—and purée in a blender.

Miso Soup with Shrimp

MAKES: 6 first course servings

There are several ways to approach this soup. The easiest is to make a plain miso soup—you can even use instant miso—and add shrimp to it. This version, however, includes lime juice, which gives the soup a delightful tang.

In a medium mixing bowl, whisk ½ cup of the dashi into the miso paste and work the mixture until it is smooth and there are no lumps. Purée the medium shrimp for about a minute in a food processor. In a heavy-bottomed pot large enough to hold the soup, combine the shrimp purée with the miso mixture and add the lime juice, leeks, and carrot. Add the remaining dashi. Place the pot on the stove over low to medium heat and simmer for 30 minutes. Strain. Just before serving, bring the broth back to a simmer and add the large shrimp. Keep at a very low simmer for 2 minutes and serve.

VARIATION: The idea of taking a basic broth, such as chicken or beef broth or miso broth made with dashi, and simmering vegetables and shrimp in it can lead to all kinds of improvisations and elegant derivatives.

10 cups dashi (see below)

3 tablespoons brown miso paste

1 pound medium shrimp, peeled
(for fortifying broth)

10 tablespoons fresh lime juice
(from about 5 limes)

greens from 3 leeks, chopped

1 carrot, peeled and chopped

6 large shrimp, boiled in the shell for
3 minutes, peeled, and well rinsed
(for serving)

Dashi

MAKES: 10 cups

This smoky, flavored fish broth is to the Japanese what basic meat and chicken broth is to European and American cooks. It takes only a few minutes to infuse shaved smoked bonito—a tuna-like fish—in seaweed-scented broth.

Put the konbu in a small pot with 10 cups of cold water. Put the pot over low to medium heat and bring to a simmer—the water should take about 15 minutes to reach a simmer—and fish out the seaweed with a pair of tongs. Bring the konbu broth back to a boil over high heat, remove from the heat, add the bonito flakes, and let steep for 1 minute. Strain—discard the bonito flakes—and let cool.

four 12-inch-long strips of konbu
(dried giant seaweed), broken in half

3 cups bonito flakes

Fat-free Shrimp Broth

MAKES: 10 cups

2 tablespoons olive oil

1 small onion, chopped coarse

1 small bulb fennel, or the stalks of the fennel, chopped coarse

1 small carrot, chopped coarse

4 quarts shrimp heads and/or shells

3 quarts water or chicken broth

3 sprigs fresh thyme (optional)

Lobster and shrimp are alike in that much of their flavor is in their shells and heads. The irony, of course, is that most Americans usually throw the heads out. It's often hard to find shrimp with heads without ordering them in advance; instead, we're left to resort to the shells we've saved up in the freezer. The flavor in shrimp shells and heads is part of an oily compound that doesn't dissolve in water the way, say, the juices in a chicken do. So the usual way of making broth—with the customary vegetables and slow cooking—isn't perfectly suited to making shrimp broth. Here's an easy way to make a broth that imparts the flavor of shrimp into any dish you include it in.

1. Heat the oil in a heavy-bottomed pot large enough to hold the soup and add the chopped vegetables. Cook over medium heat until softened but not browned, about 10 minutes. Add the shrimp heads and shells and turn the heat to high. Continue cooking over high heat while stirring around the heads and shells until the mixture smells fragrant and everything turns red, about 4 minutes.

2. Let cool a few minutes and transfer the mixture to a food processor. Chop for about 30 seconds—enough to break the heads and shells up without turning them into a purée. Put the processed mixture in a pot and add the water or broth and the thyme, if using. Bring to a gentle simmer and simmer for 1 hour—don't let the broth come to a full boil—and skim off any froth and scum that floats to the top of the pot. Strain the broth and reserve the shells and heads for shrimp butter or creamy shrimp broth.

CREAMY SHRIMP BROTH: This broth uses cream to extract the flavor and color from shrimp shells and heads. Prepare the Fat-free Shrimp Broth as directed, but substitute 3 cups heavy cream for 1 quart of the broth or water.

Shrimp Consommé

MAKES: 6 first course servings

Making any kind of consommé can be somewhat laborious because of the careful clarification and straining that's involved, but the results are phenomenal and capture the pure essence of foods like nothing else. This basic shrimp consommé is delightfully intense but the formula can be taken to any degree of obsession by making broth out of broth ad infinitum to come up with double or even triple consommé. To make double consommé, use shrimp broth instead of water or chicken broth to make Fat-free Shrimp Broth and then use that to make the consommé. Because of its richness, expense, and intense flavor, consommé is usually served in smaller portions than most soups. If you don't have consommé cups, espresso cups work beautifully. Consommé is usually served at the start of a meal, but it occasionally shows up as a little break between courses.

1. If you're using the shrimp heads and/or shells, spread them on a sheet pan and roast them in a 350°F oven until fragrant, about 25 minutes. (It's better to roast than sauté them, as in the broth on page 68, to avoid introducing oil into the clear broth.) Let cool.

2. Put the heads and/or shells in a pot large enough to hold all the ingredients and crush them with the end of French-style rolling pin or a cleaver held on end. Pour in the sherry.

3. Wash your hands thoroughly—the oil can interfere with the clarification—and combine the vegetables, tomatoes, tarragon, parsley, peppercorns, and egg whites in a large mixing bowl. Add the shrimp broth, which should be no hotter than a hot bath, into the egg white mixture. Whisk hard for a good minute to thoroughly combine and pour this mixture over the shrimp heads in the pot. Whisk some more to combine and place the pot over medium heat with the pot off-center so the broth comes to a simmer on one side only. After simmering the broth gently for 5 minutes, reposition the pot so it simmers somewhere else. Continue in this way, repositioning the pot every 5 minutes, for a total of 30 minutes, or until you can see the clear broth through the coagulated whites.

2 quarts shrimp heads and/or shells (optional)

½ cup dry fino sherry (optional)

1 bulb fennel or 3 fennel stalks, chopped coarse

1 small carrot, chopped

1 leek or small onion, chopped fine

3 tomatoes, stemmed, seeded, and chopped coarse

1 large bunch fresh tarragon, 18 leaves reserved, chopped coarse (stems included)

1 medium bunch parsley, preferably Italian flat leaf, chopped coarse (stems included)

5 peppercorns, crushed under the bottom of a heavy saucepan or skillet

3 egg whites

1 quart Fat-free Shrimp Broth (see recipe, opposite; preferably made from shrimp broth)

salt to taste

6 small shrimp, peeled, deveined, and steamed, poached, or sautéed (if sautéing, pat off any adhering oil)

4. Line a large strainer with 3 sheets of cheesecloth and run water through it to rinse out any soap or sizing. Gently ladle the broth through the cheesecloth. Season to taste with salt and ladle into warm bowls or cups. Add a small shrimp and 3 tarragon leaves to each serving.

Shrimp Consommé en Gelée

One of the only things better than hot consommé is cold consommé. Since most consommé is made with meat, and thus contains gelatin released by the meat as it cooks, cold consommé is usually a jelly. Since shrimp contains little if any gelatin, we have to add gelatin to create the same effect. The easiest way is just to add a packet (1 tablespoon) of gelatin to every 1 ½ cups of hot consommé. Soak the gelatin in 2 tablespoons of cold water for 10 minutes, and then stir it into the hot consommé until it dissolves. A more purist approach, and one that will give you more flavor, is to use a gelatinous homemade chicken broth to make the shrimp broth or consommé. The natural gelatin from the chicken broth is enough to set the consommé.

Cold consommé looks lovely served in small cups such as double espresso cups. One favorite dish is a cold poached egg topped with chopped consommé jelly; some chefs make a *brunoise* (tiny dice) of blanched vegetables to decorate the jelly and add some color and texture; and old French cookbooks extol the virtues of truffle-scented jelly. The jelly is also delicious in a small mound over a raw oyster on the half shell.

One of the easiest and most elegant ways to present a cold consommé is to serve it with crème fraîche, which adds tang and a delightful cool richness, and a small or not-so-small shrimp. The final dish can be topped with a little caviar.

Shrimp "Gazpacho"

MAKES: 6 first course servings

FOR THE GAZPACHO

3 medium tomatoes, peeled

1 regular cucumber, peeled

1 small red onion, chopped fine

1 small clove garlic, minced and crushed to a paste with the side of a chef's knife

1 red or yellow bell pepper, charred, peeled (see page 20), seeded, and diced

1 jalapeño chile, or 1 chipotle chile in adobo sauce, sauce rinsed off, or 1 dried chipotle chile, soaked for 30 minutes in warm water and drained; stemmed, seeded, and minced

1 small bunch cilantro, large stems removed, leaves and small stems chopped fine just before using

3 tablespoons extra virgin olive oil

2 tablespoons very good quality white wine vinegar, such as sherry vinegar, or 3 tablespoons fresh lime juice

1 tablespoon salt

Combining diced shrimp with a crisp, cool, and spicy gazpacho creates an obvious and naturally good combination, but when the shrimp is diced so that it's an integral part of the soup, something is lost and it's hard to perceive the shrimp flavor. When the shrimp is left in larger pieces, the gazpacho becomes almost an accompaniment or salsa instead of a genuine soup that has all the vibrancy of good gazpacho but none of the shrimp flavor. One solution to this problem is to make a gazpacho base and serve a cold shrimp sauce on the side for guests to swirl into the soup. Another solution, somewhat more elaborate, is to make a delicate shrimp mousse for the bottom of the bowls, chill it well, and then ladle the icy gazpacho over the mousse just before serving. The mousse below is closely related to a Bavarian cream in that it's made with whipped cream and a small amount of gelatin, except, of course, that it's not sweet. The base for the Bavarian cream is the Creamy Shrimp Broth on page 68.

PREPARING THE GAZPACHO

1. Cut away the sides of the tomatoes (see page 21) and cut these into dice. Work the pulp and seeds through a strainer and reserve what comes through.

2. Halve the cucumber lengthwise and use a spoon to scoop the seeds out of one half. Cut the half lengthwise into strips about ¼-inch wide. Slice the strips crosswise to make ¼-inch dice. Save the remaining cucumber half for another use.

3. Combine all the vegetables, the tomato pulp, the cilantro, the oil, the vinegar, and the salt in a mixing bowl and stir thoroughly. Refrigerate for 2 hours—the salt will draw the liquid out of the vegetables and provide the liquid for the gazpacho.

PREPARING THE BAVARIAN MOUSSE:

1. In a medium saucepan, gently heat the shrimp broth until it is slightly
   warmer than room temperature and add the gelatin and its soaking
   liquid, stirring until the gelatin is completely dissolved. In a mixing
   bowl, combine the tarragon with the cream and whip to soft peaks
   with a whisk (the cream will droop off the end of the whisk when you
   hold it horizontally). Use a rubber spatula to fold the cream into the
   warm broth mixture, and season with salt to taste. Ladle ¼ cup of the
   mixture into each of 6 well-chilled deep soup bowls and refrigerate
   for at least an hour until the mixture sets. The mousse can be prepared
   1 day ahead.

2. Spoon the gazpacho into each of the mousse-lined bowls and serve.

FOR THE MOUSSE

¾ cup Creamy Shrimp Broth
   (see page 68)

½ packet unflavored gelatin (1 ½
   teaspoons), soaked for 15 minutes
   in 3 tablespoons cold water

leaves from 2 sprigs tarragon, chopped
   fine just before using

½ cup heavy cream

salt to taste

Shrimp Tomatillo Soup

MAKES: 6 first course servings

The idea for this soup comes from those lovely tangy green enchiladas served in Mexican restaurants in southern California. Tomatillos aren't green tomatoes but they are closely related to gooseberries—they're wrapped in the same papery sheath.

1. In a pot large enough to hold the soup, cook the onion and garlic in the oil over medium heat. Stir every minute or so and adjust the heat so the onions turn shiny but don't brown, about 10 minutes. Add the chiles and tomatillos. (If you're using fresh tomatillos, cut them in half.) Add the broth or water, cover the pot, and simmer for 10 minutes for canned tomatillos, 15 minutes for fresh tomatillos.

2. Purée the soup with an immersion blender or regular blender. If you want it smooth, work the soup through a food mill or coarse strainer before putting it back in the pot. Bring the soup back to a simmer and add the shrimp. Simmer for about 3 minutes and season to taste with salt and pepper. Pass tortilla strips, if using (see below), the sour cream, and the cheese at the table.

FRYING TORTILLA STRIPS: Cut the tortillas in half and then cut the halves, on a bias, into 1/3-inch strips. Heat the oil in a heavy saucepan large enough so the oil doesn't come more than halfway up the sides. When the oil begins to ripple, at about 375°F, add one of the strips. It should stay on the surface and be immediately surrounded with bubbles; if this doesn't happen, wait for the oil to get hotter and try again. Add the tortillas, half at a time, and fry for about 1 minute, until pale brown. Keep in mind that the strips continue to darken after you take them out of the oil. Take the strips out of the oil with a spider utensil, skimmer, or slotted spoon and drain them on paper towels.

1 medium white or yellow onion, chopped fine

2 cloves garlic, minced

2 tablespoons olive oil or canola oil

1 dried chipotle chile, soaked for 30 minutes in warm water and drained, or 1 canned chipotle chile in adobo sauce, or 2 jalapeño chiles; stemmed, seeded and chopped fine

2 fresh poblano chiles, charred, peeled (see page 20), seeded, and chopped fine

three 13-ounce cans tomatillos, drained, or 2 pounds fresh tomatillos, sheaths removed

2 cups shrimp broth, water, or chicken broth

18 to 24 large shrimp, peeled and deveined (deveining optional)

salt and pepper to taste

FOR THE GARNITURE

3 corn tortillas (optional)

3 cups vegetable oil (for the optional tortillas)

1 pint sour cream

1/2 pound mild cheese such as Monterey Jack or mild cheddar, grated coarse

stews

Shrimp Mole

MAKES: 6 main course servings

10 dried mulato chiles

6 dried ancho chiles

6 dried pasilla chiles

1 chipotle chile, either dried or canned in adobo sauce

2 tablespoons sesame seeds

½ teaspoon coriander seeds

¼ cup almonds with their skins

1 medium onion, chopped

2 cloves garlic, chopped

2 tablespoons vegetable oil

2 tomatoes, stemmed and chopped

1 quart shrimp broth or chicken broth

¼ cup raisins

¼ teaspoon ground cloves

½ teaspoon ground cinnamon

2 teaspoons sugar, or more to taste

1 tablespoon sherry vinegar, or more to taste

30 large or 24 jumbo shrimp, peeled and deveined (deveining optional)

salt and pepper to taste

FOR SERVING

boiled or steamed rice

sour cream

tortillas

lime wedges

Most Americans associate moles with chocolate, but chocolate often plays little if any part in flavoring a mole, since chiles are the primary flavor component. The complex flavor of dried chiles allows for endless improvisation and combinations resulting in different flavor nuances. Some of the more exotic dried chiles can be hard to track down and may require a mail order, but once you have them on hand, they'll keep, tightly wrapped, for a year or even longer in the freezer. To reconstitute dried chiles after they've been toasted, soak them in a bowl of warm water for about 30 minutes or until they become pliable. Cut them in half lengthwise, rinse out the seeds, and discard the water, which is often bitter. The chile is then ready to use.

1. Put the chiles, except the canned chipotle, if using, in a cast-iron skillet over medium heat. Rearrange them every couple of minutes and turn them over so they are all roasted equally, about 5 minutes. When they are fragrant and turn a deeper red, let cool and soak in a bowl with enough water to cover until soft and pliable, about 30 minutes; put a plate over them to keep them submerged. If you're using a dried chipotle chile, soak it until soft, about 30 minutes (chipotles don't need toasting to bring out their aroma). Take the chiles out of the pan and stir in the sesame seeds, toasting for about 2 minutes over medium heat, until they smell fragrant. Toast the coriander seeds in the same way and for about the same time; toast the almonds in this way for about 7 minutes, stirring every 30 seconds or so. Reserve all the toasted ingredients. If you're using a canned chipotle chile, rinse off the adobo sauce. Cut the stems off the chiles and halve them lengthwise. Rinse out the seeds and chop the chiles coarsely.

2. In a heavy-bottomed pot large enough to hold the finished mole, cook the onion and garlic in the oil over medium heat until translucent, about 10 minutes. Add the tomatoes and 2 cups of the broth and simmer for about 7 minutes. Pour half the mixture into a blender and add the toasted seeds, almonds, raisins, chiles, and ground spices. Purée

for 1 minute and strain into a clean pot. Purée the remaining onion
mixture with the rest of the broth and combine the two batches.

3. Just before serving, bring the mole mixture to a simmer, add the
sugar, vinegar, and shrimp. Simmer for 2 to 3 minutes, season to taste
with salt and pepper, and serve. Mole is best served accompanied by
simple boiled or steamed rice, sour cream, tortillas, and lime wedges.

Thai Shrimp Curry

MAKES: 6 main course servings

Unlike Indian curry, which is a powder, Thai curry is a paste made by working together various herbs and chiles in a mortar and pestle for most of a day; a food processor or blender just doesn't do the job. You can buy preground Thai curry, but it never has the same flavor as fresh. The solution is to purée the flavorful ingredients with some broth or water.

The main ingredients that give Thai food its character are chiles; kaffir lime leaves; cilantro; lemongrass; and galangal (a pine-like rhizome similar to ginger root, but with a very different flavor). The soul of Thai curries and most Thai dishes is provided by fish sauce, which is made by fermenting fish in the sun for many months. Shrimp paste, made by subjecting shrimp to a similar process, is so pungent that many western cooks leave it out of dishes for fear of their houses smelling like a fish stall in August.

Thai curries are notoriously hot—green is hotter than red—and require a shocking number of chiles. This recipe strays from traditional versions in that it contains poblano chiles, normally associated with Mexican cooking, because they provide plenty of flavor without overwhelming the dish with heat.

1. Combine the chiles, lemongrass, shallots, garlic, cilantro, 2 of the kaffir lime leaves, the galangal, the spices, and 1 cup of the broth in a food processor. Purée for 1 minute. If the mixture gets too stiff to process, add more broth. Transfer the mixture to a saucepan and bring to a simmer over medium heat. Simmer gently for 5 minutes, remove from the heat, and work the mixture through a strainer into a clean pot large enough to hold the finished curry.

2. Add the rest of the ingredients except the shrimp and including any remaining broth, and return to a simmer. Simmer for 2 to 7 minutes until slightly thickened. Add the shrimp and continue to simmer for another 3 minutes. If the curry needs salt, add more fish sauce, which will provide the salt and savor as well. Serve with plenty of steamed jasmine or basmati rice.

3 poblano chiles, charred, peeled (see page 20), stemmed, seeded, and chopped

2 jalapeño chiles or 2 Thai "bird" chiles, stemmed, seeded, and chopped (optional)

1 stalk lemongrass, 6 inches of white soft part sliced as thin as possible

3 shallots, chopped

3 cloves garlic, chopped

1 medium bunch cilantro, chopped coarse, stems included

8 kaffir lime leaves

one 1-inch piece of galangal, sliced as thin as possible (optional)

1 teaspoon ground coriander

½ teaspoon ground cumin

½ teaspoon ground white pepper

2 cups shrimp broth, chicken broth, or water

¼ cup Thai fish sauce, or more to taste

½ cup basil leaves, preferably small "holy" basil or basilico piccolo

1 cup unsweetened coconut milk (preferably a Thai brand)

3 tablespoons fresh lime juice

30 large or 24 jumbo shrimp, peeled and deveined (deveining optional)

steamed jasmine or basmati rice (for serving)

12 stalks thick green or white asparagus

10 ounces cultivated mushrooms, preferably cremini

1/2 cup baby peas (frozen are fine)

2/3 pound fresh fava beans in the husk or frozen fava beans, husked (optional)

1 ounce dried morel mushrooms (optional)

2 large artichokes (optional)

1/2 lemon (for the optional artichokes)

1/3 pound green beans, preferably French-style *haricots verts*, ends snapped off

2 cups spinach leaves

1/4 cup salt (for blanching vegetables)

18 to 24 pearl onions (optional)

1 cup homemade chicken broth or water if you're using pearl onions, 1/4 cup broth or water if you're not

1 small bunch chives

1 small bunch parsley, large stems removed

1 small bunch chervil

leaves from 2 sprigs tarragon

1/2 cup heavy cream

24 large or 18 jumbo shrimp for first courses or 20 large or 16 jumbo shrimp for main courses

salt and pepper to taste

Shrimp Fricassée with Spring Vegetables

MAKES: 6 first course or 4 main course servings

While this is one of those dishes that you put together based on what shows up at your local farmers' market, there are usually a few standbys that you can count on, such as green beans, asparagus, and spinach. Frozen peas, provided you don't boil them as suggested on the package, are the only frozen vegetable that's consistently better than fresh. Fresh baby peas, not the starchy monsters found year-round, seem to be in season only for a couple of weeks in May or June.

The sauce presented here is flavored with chervil, tarragon, parsley, and chives—the classic herb mixture the French call fines herbes—but you can also use only one herb; just parsley is fine as long as it's chopped at the last minute and not allowed to sit on the kitchen counter where it will quickly lose its aroma. The essence of the sauce comes from the morel mushrooms, which can be replaced by wild mushrooms if they are available and affordable. The puff pastry squares are completely optional but they give this dish a festive elegance and a delightful contrasting crunch.

EARLY ON THE DAY OF SERVING:

1. Cut 1 inch off the ends of the asparagus spears and discard. Use a vegetable peeler to peel away the fibrous skin of each spear, starting at the base of the flower and working all the way to the end of the spear. Cut each spear into three 3-inch-long sections.

2. Rinse the mushrooms and cut off the very end of the stem if it's dark or crusty. Shuck or thaw the peas, and shuck the fava beans, if using fresh ones.

3. In a very small bowl, soak the morel mushrooms in just enough water to cover 1/3 of the way up their sides. Press down on them every 10 minutes and move them around until they're completely soft, about 30 minutes total. Squeeze the morels and reserve any liquid that comes out, along with the soaking liquid, in the bowl. Place the morels in another small bowl.

4. If using the artichokes, cut the stems and leaves off by turning them as shown on page 85. Boil the cores in enough water to cover by about an inch (if they bob up, put a small plate over them) until a knife penetrates the base with just moderate pressure, about 10 minutes. Drain and rub with the lemon half.

5. Bring about 6 quarts of water to a rapid boil. Use a pot that you can reach into with a large strainer or spider utensil in order to fish out the vegetables as you blanch them. Add the ¼ cup salt.

6. Place the green beans in the boiling water and boil until tender, about 5 minutes. Scoop them out with a strainer, spider utensil, or slotted spoon and transfer them to a colander in the sink. Rinse immediately with cold water until cool and drain. Transfer to a clean bowl.

7. Add the asparagus sections to the water and boil until tender, about 3 minutes. Scoop out into the colander and rinse with cold water until cool.

8. Add the fava beans to the water, boil for 1 minute, scoop out, and rinse with cold water in the colander.

9. Add the peas, boil them for about 1 minute, drain, and rinse. Add the spinach leaves, stir them around in the water until they go limp—just a few seconds—and transfer to the colander. Rinse with cold water.

10. If using the pearl onions, add them to the boiling water, boil for 2 minutes, and rinse.

11. Peel the fava beans and pearl onions with a paring knife and your thumbnail. Scoop the chokes out of the artichoke bottoms and cut each of the bottoms into 6 wedges.

12. If you're not finishing the fricassée right away, squeeze the lemon into a small bowl and toss the artichoke bottoms in the juice so the artichokes won't turn gray. Cover all the vegetables and refrigerate.

JUST BEFORE SERVING:

1. Put the peeled pearl onions in a saucepan with ¾ cup of the chicken broth or water. Cover the pot and cook over low to medium heat for 15 minutes. Slice the mushrooms and put them in the saucepan with the onions, or in a saucepan large enough to hold the entire stew if you're not using the onions, with the remaining ¼ cup chicken broth or water. Cover the pan and cook over low heat for 5 minutes. While the mushrooms are cooking, finely chop the herbs. Stir the herbs into the saucepan and add the cream. Add the spinach leaves and the shrimp and put the other vegetables on top. As you add the vegetables, season with salt and freshly ground pepper to taste. Cover the pot and steam over medium heat for 3 minutes.

2. Spoon the vegetables and shrimp into heated soup plates and spoon the sauce over them, coating the vegetables and shrimp. If you like, garnish each plate with sprig of chervil.

OPTIONAL VARIATION

1 pound puff pastry (made with all butter)

1 egg

salt

OPTIONAL VARIATION: If you want to serve this dish in a puff pastry square—an elegant touch—roll the pastry into a sheet between ⅛- and ¼-inch thick and large enough to make 4 or 6 squares about 3 inches on each side. Chill the puff pastry in the freezer long enough for it to be firm but not too hard to cut—this is so you don't crimp it when you cut the squares—and cut out the squares. With the tip of a knife, make a series of lines diagonally across each of the squares, about 1/16-inch deep. Beat the egg with a big pinch of salt and brush the squares with the beaten egg. Don't let any of the egg drip down the sides. Freeze the squares and preheat the oven to 450° F. Bake the squares until fully puffed and lightly browned, about 15 minutes, and turn the oven down to 275° F. Continue baking for 20 minutes more. Let cool and cut in half through the sides. Pull out and discard any raw dough in the middle. Serve the fricassée in between the 2 halves.

How to "Turn" Artichokes

To get to the meaty core or "heart" of an artichoke, you must first remove the stem and leaves.

A: Cut off the stem at the base of the artichoke.

B: With a sharp paring knife held perpendicular to the base of the artichoke, rotate the artichoke so the outermost leaves come away.

C and D: Continue to rotate as necessary to reveal the white inner core of the artichoke. It's better to cut less deeply and have to rotate more than it is to cut too deeply at the start and waste some of the artichoke.

E: Rotate the artichoke against your knife to cut any green away from the base.

F: Trim off any green that's left from the "turning."

G: Cut the base away from the leaves. Don't cut too close to the base; it's better to err in favor of the leaves, since you can always trim them away.

H: Trim off the ends of the leaves all around the base.

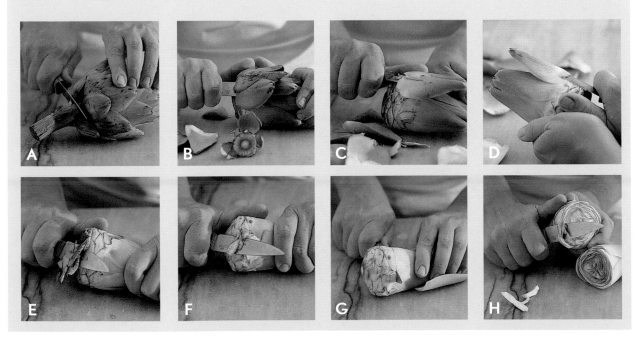

Shrimp with Truffles and Hazelnut Oil

MAKES: 4 first course servings

This is a stunning little dish. If you don't have hazelnut oil, you can skip it—truffles infused in cream have flavor enough—but the hazelnut oil does add an exciting note.

3/4 cup heavy cream

1 small black winter truffle (see page 39), chopped

1 teaspoon Dijon mustard

3 tablespoons hazelnut oil made from roasted nuts (LeBlanc is a good brand)

16 large shrimp, peeled and deveined

salt and pepper to taste

1. Bring the cream to a simmer over medium heat in a small saucepan and simmer until it thickens slightly, about 5 minutes. Add the truffle. Cover the saucepan and let it sit, off the heat, for 15 minutes, to infuse the aroma of the truffle. Whisk in the mustard and the hazelnut oil— add the oil a teaspoon at a time so it emulsifies with the cream—and add the shrimp. Put the mixture over medium heat, stirring almost constantly, until the shrimp turns orange, about 3 minutes. If the sauce has gotten too thick, thin it with a little water or cream. Season to taste with salt and pepper. Arrange 4 shrimp each on 4 heated plates.

VARIATION: To make 6 dainty but very satisfying hors d'oeuvres called *bouchées* (bites), roll out a sheet of puff pastry to between 1/16- and 1/8-inch thick. Use a fluted cookie cutter to cut out twelve 1 1/2-inch-wide rounds. Use a 1-inch cookie cutter to cut a smaller round out of 6 of the 1 1/2-inch rounds. This will leave you with six 1 1/2-inch rounds, six 1-inch rounds, and 6 rings. Brush the 6 larger rounds with water and place a ring on each one. Brush the rings and the smaller rounds with beaten egg—don't let any drip down the sides—and chill for 20 minutes. Preheat the oven to 450°F. Cut 3 medium shrimp into tiny dice and combine them with 1/3 of the recipe for the sauce given above. Season with salt and pepper to taste. Bake the *bouchées* until puffed and golden brown, about 15 minutes, and then turn down the heat to 300°F and bake for 15 minutes more to cook them through. Put the shrimp mixture in the little cups, sprinkle with some julienned truffles, and top with the lids.

Shrimp with Truffles and Morels

MAKES: 4 first course servings

Dried morels have a lovely affinity with truffles and while they're not inexpensive, they seem to be compared with truffles, and they go a long way in stretching the truffles' flavor. Fresh morels, strangely, have less of the smoky truffle-like flavor than the dried variety.

1. If you're using the puff pastry, roll the sheet into four 3- x 1 ½-inch rectangles about ⅛-inch thick and make a series of diagonal lines about ¼-inch apart across the top of the rectangles. Beat the egg with a teaspoon of water and brush it on the rectangles. Don't let any of the egg mixture drip down the sides of the pastry or it may prevent the pastry from rising. Freeze the rectangles for 15 minutes.

2. Preheat the oven to 425°F. Sprinkle a sheet pan with cold water, place the rectangles on top, and bake until pale brown and puffed, about 12 minutes. Turn the oven down to 250°F and bake for 30 minutes more to cook the pastry all the way through. Let cool slightly and cut the rectangles in half through the sides. Pull out and discard any raw dough in the middle.

3. In a medium saucepan, simmer the cream over medium heat until it thickens slightly, about 5 minutes. Squeeze the morels over the bowl they soaked in and gently transfer the soaking liquid into the cream, leaving any dirt or grit behind in the bowl. Simmer the cream again until it has the consistency you like—just slightly thicker than cold heavy cream is usually about right. Add the truffle to the cream. Take the cream off the heat and cover the saucepan; let the sauce sit for 20 minutes for the truffle to infuse.

4. Whisk in the mustard and hazelnut oil and add the morels. Just before you're ready to serve, put the shrimp in the sauce and heat gently just long enough to cook through the shrimp, about 3 minutes. Season to taste with salt and pepper. If you're using the puff pastry, arrange the shrimp, truffles, morels, and sauce on the bottom halves of the pastry on heated plates and cover with the top halves.

12 ounces puff pastry (optional)

1 egg yolk (for the puff pastry)

¾ cup heavy cream

12 dried morels, soaked in ¼ cup water for 30 minutes

1 small black winter truffle (see page 39), chopped

1 teaspoon Dijon mustard

3 tablespoons hazelnut oil made from roasted nuts (LeBlanc is a good brand)

16 large shrimp, peeled, and deveined

salt and pepper to taste

Shrimp Tagine

Makes 6 main course servings

Moroccan cooking is complex and very underappreciated. This recipe derives from many like it, but extracts the best flavors and components of each. To learn more about authentic Moroccan cooking, consult Paula Wolfert's Couscous and Other Good Food from Morocco.

1 medium onion, chopped fine

4 medium carrots, peeled and sliced

3 cloves garlic, chopped

3 tablespoons butter

one 1-inch piece fresh ginger, peeled and grated fine

1 teaspoon cumin

½ teaspoon cinnamon

1 teaspoon ground turmeric or 1 tablespoon fresh turmeric, grated

¼ teaspoon ground cloves

½ teaspoon saffron threads, soaked for 30 minutes in 1 tablespoon water

6 tomatoes, peeled (see page 21), stemmed, seeded, and chopped

1 small bunch cilantro, large stems removed

leaves from 1 small bunch mint

3 tablespoons golden raisins (sultanas)

3 tablespoons slivered almonds, toasted in a 350°F oven until pale brown, about 12 minutes

½ preserved lemon, cut into ¼-inch dice (about 2 tablespoons after dicing), rinsed in a strainer (optional; these are available in most gourmet grocery stores)

30 large or 18 jumbo shrimp, peeled and deveined (deveining optional)

¾ to 1 cup bottled harissa sauce, for serving

In a heavy-bottomed pot large enough to hold the whole tagine, cook the onion, carrots, and garlic in the butter over medium heat until the onion is translucent and the carrots soft, about 15 minutes. Add the ginger, cumin, cinnamon, turmeric, cloves, and saffron with its soaking liquid to the carrot mixture. Gently stir the mixture—avoid breaking up the carrots—and cook over low to medium heat for about 2 minutes more. Add the tomatoes, cover the pot, and simmer on low heat, covered, for 10 minutes more. Chop the cilantro and mint and stir into the sauce with the raisins, almonds, preserved lemon, if using, and shrimp. Simmer for 2 to 3 minutes. Serve with couscous or rice and harissa sauce.

Goan-style Shrimp "Curry"

MAKES: 4 main course servings

3 tablespoons Goan Red Spice Paste, or more to taste (see recipe, opposite)

one 15-ounce can unsweetened coconut milk

1 medium bunch cilantro, large stems removed, leaves and small stems chopped fine

28 large or 16 jumbo shrimp, peeled and deveined (deveining optional)

salt to taste

2 tablespoons fresh lime juice

steamed or boiled basmati rice (for serving)

India has so many miles of coastline that practically every region has some version of shrimp simmered in curry and yogurt, cream, or coconut milk. What distinguishes all authentic Indian recipes, however, is the absence of curry powder; to an Indian cook, using a premixed curry would be akin to a French cook using a premixed bottle of dried herbs for every dish. Many Goan recipes—Goa was a Portuguese colony on India's west coast—contain a spice paste that's made in advance and preserved with vinegar. It gives a delightful tangy complexity to many Indian stews, not just those made with shrimp, and once you have it on hand—it keeps for months—you can throw together a dish in minutes.

In a medium-sized pot, combine the spice paste, coconut milk, and cilantro and bring to a gentle simmer. Add the shrimp and simmer for 2 to 3 minutes. Add salt to taste. Sprinkle with lime juice. Serve with basmati rice.

Goan Red Spice Paste

MAKES: about 2 1/2 cups

Heat the ghee or oil over low to medium heat in a small sauté pan and add the onions and garlic. Stir until the onion is translucent but not yet brown—about 7 minutes. Add the rest of the ingredients except the vinegar and stir on the heat for about 3 minutes to coax the flavor out of the spices. Add the vinegar and remove from the heat. When the mixture has cooled, purée it in a blender for about a minute. The spice paste will keep for months in the refrigerator.

1/4 cup ghee (see page 94) or
   vegetable oil

2 medium onions, chopped fine

6 cloves garlic, minced

8 red Thai "bird" chiles, stemmed,
   seeded, and chopped fine

2 teaspoons ground cumin

2 teaspoons ground cardamom

1 teaspoon ground cinnamon

4 teaspoons ground turmeric

4 teaspoons ground coriander seeds

1 teaspoon ground cloves

4 teaspoons freshly ground black pepper

3 tablespoons paprika

two 4-inch pieces fresh ginger, peeled
   and grated fine

1 cup good quality wine vinegar

Ghee

MAKES: 1 ½ cups

1 pound (4 sticks) unsalted butter

In western cooking, ghee is called beurre noisette. *Some people mistake ghee for clarified butter—which it is—but it's clarified butter made in a specific way. The trick to making ghee is to cook the butter—which must be unsalted—very slowly until the milk solids caramelize in brown specks that cling to the sides and bottom of the saucepan and float around in the butter. When the butter's at this stage, it must be immediately cooled and strained. Clarified butter lasts for months when well covered in the refrigerator.*

Put the butter in a small, heavy-bottomed saucepan over medium heat. In about 10 minutes it will be frothy and bubbling. When the froth starts to subside slightly, turn down the heat to low and watch the butter closely. Prepare a bowl of cold water large enough to fit the bottom of the saucepan. As the butter cooks, check the bottom of the saucepan by tilting it and seeing if any specks of brown coagulated milk solids are adhering to it. After 15 to 20 minutes total cooking time you'll see the milk solids coagulate into white specks and within a minute or two these specks will turn pale brown and then deep brown. As soon as they turn deep brown, dip the bottom of the saucepan in the bowl of cold water for a few seconds to stop the cooking. Pass the butter through a strainer lined with a triple layer of cheesecloth, paper towels, or a clean kitchen towel (not terrycloth, however, or it will absorb too much butter). The butter should have a lovely nutty fragrance. Store, well covered, in the refrigerator.

Velvet Shrimp with Spices, Cashews, and Ghee

MAKES: 4 main course servings

This dish is somewhat rich because of the ghee. If you want to lighten it, replace the cream with plain yogurt—preferably yogurt you've drained overnight to thicken—and leave the ghee out entirely. But the rich nuttiness of the ghee, combined with the nuttiness of the cashews, is hard to beat.

In a small, heavy-bottomed pot large enough to hold the stew, cook the onions, garlic, and ginger in 2 tablespoons ghee or vegetable oil until translucent, about 6 to 8 minutes. Stir in the spice paste and cook for 3 minutes more. Add half the cashews and the heavy cream and cook just long enough to heat the cream to the temperature of a hot bath. (If the cream is cold it will turn to butter in the blender; if it's too hot, it will try to shoot out the top.) Pour this mixture into a blender and purée for about a minute. Strain the mixture back into the pot and bring to a gentle simmer. Stir in the remaining ghee, if you're using it, the remaining cashews, and the shrimp. Simmer for about 3 minutes. Season to taste with salt and pepper. Serve with basmati rice.

1 medium onion, chopped fine

2 cloves garlic, chopped

one 1-inch piece fresh ginger, peeled and grated fine

⅓ cup ghee (see recipe, opposite) or 2 tablespoons vegetable oil

3 tablespoons Goan Spice Paste, or more to taste (see page 93)

1 cup roasted cashews

1 ½ cups heavy cream or 2 cups yogurt, drained for an hour in a cheesecloth-lined strainer, or 1 cup Greek-style yogurt

24 large or 16 jumbo shrimp, peeled and deveined (deveining optional)

salt and pepper to taste

steamed or boiled basmati rice (for serving)

one 4-pound chicken or 2 single bone-in chicken breasts and 2 chicken thighs with drumsticks

24 medium shrimp, peeled and deveined (with heads unless you have reserved heads or Creamy Shrimp Broth)

2 cups Creamy Shrimp Broth (see page 68) or heads from 24 medium shrimp

2 tablespoons olive oil (for heads)

4 tomatoes, stemmed and chopped

½ teaspoon fresh or dried thyme leaves

1 cup heavy cream

salt and pepper to taste

3 tablespoons butter

1 medium onion, chopped fine

½ teaspoon saffron threads, soaked in 1 tablespoon water (optional)

leaves from 4 sprigs fresh tarragon, chopped just before using

1 cup or one 10-ounce package pearl onions (optional), boiled for 1 minute and peeled

1 tablespoon butter (for the onions)

10 ounces cultivated mushrooms, preferably small button-type cremini

1 tablespoon butter (for the mushrooms)

Chicken with Shrimp

MAKES: 4 main course servings

One of France's great dishes, or more specifically Lyon's, is Poulet aux Ecrevisses *(Chicken with Crayfish). Two hundred years ago, there were more such dishes—seafood combined with chicken—that provided a means of extending the flavor of rare and expensive ingredients with something relatively neutral such as chicken. The same method used for crayfish works just as well with shrimp. Be sure to buy wild Gulf shrimp for this dish, and look for shrimp broth or shrimp with heads with which to make the broth.*

1. If you're starting with a whole chicken, cut away the thighs and drumsticks, leaving the thighs attached to the drumsticks. Stand the chicken on end with the larger opening up, and with a large knife cut down through it, separating the back and double breast. Discard the back or save it for broth. Place the double breast skin side down on a cutting board and with the large knife held vertically, cut through the cartilage that joins the two single breasts. Cut through and separate the breasts. Set aside.

2. If you don't have Creamy Shrimp Broth, make it using reserved shrimp heads or the heads from the shrimp you're cooking for the dish. Heat the olive oil in a heavy skillet over high heat until it ripples, and toss in the heads. Stir over high heat for about 5 minutes until bright red and fragrant. Let cool and chop for 1 minute in a food processor. Combine with the tomatoes, thyme, and heavy cream in a saucepan and simmer gently for 20 minutes. Strain through a coarse strainer and again through a fine strainer. Reserve.

3. Season the chicken breasts and thighs with salt and pepper and cook them in the butter in a sauté pan just large enough to hold them in a single layer over medium heat, skin side down, for about 10 minutes, or until lightly browned. Turn and cook on the other side for about 5 minutes more—the chicken shouldn't be completely cooked at this point. Transfer the chicken to a plate and discard all but a tablespoon of the fat left in the sauté pan (if it's burnt, pour it all out and replace it

with 1 tablespoon fresh butter) and add the chopped onion. Cook over medium heat until translucent, about 10 minutes.

4. Add the reserved shrimp head mixture or the Creamy Shrimp Broth to the sauté pan and add the saffron, its soaking liquid, and the tarragon and let the mixture sit off the heat until you're close to serving.

5. While the chicken is cooking, put the pearl onions (if using) in a pan large enough to hold them in a single layer and add enough water to come halfway up their sides. Partially cover the pan and bring to a medium simmer. Simmer for about 15 minutes—watch closely so the water doesn't run dry and burn the onions and add more water as needed—until the onions are easily pierced with a knife. It there's water still left in the pan, turn the heat to high and boil away the water. To brown the onions, add a tablespoon of butter to the pan and sauté them lightly. If the mushroom caps are larger than 1 inch across, cut them through the top into quarters. Sauté in butter in another pan until any water they release evaporates and they turn deep brown.

6. Within 10 minutes of serving, put the chicken back in the sauté pan, skin side up, with the sauce. Add the pearl onions and mushrooms, and cover the pan. Bring to a gentle simmer and simmer for 5 to 10 minutes or until the chicken springs back when you press on it with your finger. Season the sauce to taste with salt and pepper. Put the chicken on heated plates and add the shrimp to the sauce. Simmer for 2 minutes and spoon the shrimp and sauce over the chicken.

Ideas for Making Shrimp Stews: How to Improvise

The techniques used for making shrimp stews are the same throughout the world, with only minor variations in technique but with big variations in the ingredients used. There's a systematic logic to making a shrimp stew that involves a series of steps, although not all the steps are used all the time. The ingredients used for each of the steps give the dish its regional or national identity.

Steps for an improvised shrimp stew:

1. Marinating
2. Presautéing (cooking fat)
3. Cooking of aromatic ingredients, usually vegetables
4. Adding liquid to the aromatic ingredients
5. Adding additional ingredients to hot liquid according to their cooking times
6. Adding thickeners and/or flavorful finishers to the liquid near the end of cooking
7. Using enricheners such as cream, coconut milk, or shrimp butter
8. Garnishing the final dish

INGREDIENTS FOR SHRIMP STEWS AND SOUPS

	Marinades	Cooking Fat	Aromatic Ingredients	Simmering Liquids
THAILAND	lemongrass, garlic, shallots, Thai curry pastes, Thai chiles, fish sauce	peanut oil, coconut oil	same as marinade ingredients; kaffir lime leaves, cilantro	water, broth, coconut milk, Thai fish sauce, shrimp head broth
CHINA	ginger, garlic, scallions, rice wine, sherry, soy sauce	peanut oil, vegetable oil	same as solid marinade ingredients	rice wine or sherry, soy sauce, sesame oil
BRAZIL	garlic, ginger, chiles, cumin, cilantro	dende oil, peanut oil, butter	onions, garlic, chiles (habanero, mirasol, jalapeño), achiote oil	coconut milk, tomatoes, beer, wine, shrimp head broth, lemon juice
FRANCE	white wine, lemon juice, olive oil, parsley, chervil, tarragon, bay leaves, thyme, onions	butter, olive oil, goose fat, duck fat	*mirepoix* (mix of onions, carrots, celery) shallots, garlic, ham	white wine, vermouth, cider, tomatoes, fish broth, shrimp head broth, clam or mussel cooking liquid
ITALY	white wine, vermouth, garlic, olive oil, oregano, basil, marjoram, bay leaves, mint, fennel	olive oil, butter, rendered pancetta, lard, prosciutto fat	onions, garlic, pancetta, prosciutto, tomatoes, herbs, sofrito, fennel	white wine, vermouth, tomato sauce, fish broth, shrimp head broth, clam or mussel cooking liquid
INDIA	turmeric, ginger, chiles, ajowan (carom) seeds	ghee, vegetable oil	onions, garlic, poppy seeds, cumin, coriander, paprika, chiles, ginger, cardamom, cinnamon, curry leaves	coconut milk, yogurt, tomatoes, cream, shrimp head broth
SPAIN	olive oil, thyme, garlic	olive oil, rendered pork fat	Catalan *sofregit*, Castilian *sofrito*; onions, leeks, tomatoes, fresh and dried hot peppers	water, fish broth, shrimp head broth, wine, Pernod (pastis), cognac or brandy, rum, sherry
MEXICO	Mexican oregano, epazote, onions, garlic, fresh chiles	butter, vegetable oil	onions, garlic, chiles, carrots	tomatoes, tomatillos, fish broth, shrimp head broth
JAPAN	sake, mirin, dashi flakes		ginger, garlic, sesame oil	dashi, sake

	Simmering Ingredients	Thickeners/ Finishers	Enricheners	Garnishes
THAILAND	kaffir lime leaves, cilantro, mint, holy basil, tomatoes, pineapple, straw mushrooms, snow peas, cucumbers	green, yellow, or red Thai curries	coconut milk	chopped scallions, peanuts, cilantro
CHINA	crispy vegetables such as snow peas, green beans, water chestnuts	cornstarch		chopped scallions
BRAZIL	dried shrimp, ginger	ground peanuts or cashews, cornstarch	coconut milk	chopped cilantro, parsley, dill
FRANCE	green vegetable such as green beans, spinach, Swiss chard; root vegetables such as turnips, celeriac, carrots, often julienned or "turned"	flour (*roux* or *beurre manié*), cornstarch, arrowroot, vegetable purées, butter, reduced cream, egg yolks	cream, butter, shrimp butter, sea urchin roe, scallop roe, lobster coral	chopped parsley, chervil, chives, tarragon
ITALY	dried porcini mushrooms, green vegetables, fennel	flour, vegetable purées	cream	chopped parsley, basil (chopped or in pesto), oregano, mint
INDIA	almonds, tamarind	ground poppy seeds, vegetable or legume (especially bean and lentil) purées, ground nuts	coconut milk, cream, yogurt, reduced milk	chopped cilantro, chiles
SPAIN	artichokes, green beans, tomatoes, cinnamon, allspice, paprika, peas, mushrooms, potatoes, rice, saffron, white beans, fava beans	toasted bread, picada (sauce made of bread peppers, garlic, and ground hazelnuts or almonds), romesco (similar to picada but with vinegar)	olive oil (usually contained in a sauce)	chopped parsley, pitted olives, toasted pine nuts, raisins
MEXICO	corn, cinnamon, cumin, chocolate, dried chiles	corn purée, ground pumpkin seeds, ground almonds	fresh cheese, cream, sour cream	raisins, pomegranate seeds
JAPAN	mushrooms, seaweed		shiso leaves, yuzu rind, shiitake mushrooms	

Seafood Fricassee

MAKES: 4 main course servings

16 mussels (some of which can be green New Zealand mussels for color)

8 littleneck clams

½ pound New Zealand cockles

4 large sea scallops

4 oysters

1 shallot, minced

½ cup dry white wine

4 jumbo shrimp, peeled and deveined (deveining optional)

1 small bunch chives, minced

1 small bunch parsley, large stems removed, leaves and small stems minced

½ cup heavy cream

4 tablespoons unsalted cold butter, cut into tablespoon slices (optional)

salt (if necessary) and pepper to taste

This is one of those dishes that lends itself to limitless improvisation. The trick is to understand how various shellfish cook and how each of them contributes to the whole, so if you don't have one or two, you can make do with the others. It's helpful to have shrimp broth for this recipe, but if you don't, the other shellfish provide plenty of flavorful liquid with which to make the sauce.

1. Scrub the mussels and clams with a stiff brush. Rinse off the cockles in a colander. Remove the little side muscles from the scallops and cut them in half crosswise into 2 disks. Shuck the oysters. Keep everything cold until about 20 minutes before you're ready to serve.

2. Combine the shallot and white wine in a wide, lidded pan that's large enough to hold all the shellfish. Cover the pan and simmer for 5 minutes over medium heat. Add the clams, simmer for 5 minutes, covered, and add the mussels. Cover the pan. Simmer for 3 minutes and add the cockles and shrimp. Cover and simmer until the cockles, mussels, and clams all open, about 5 minutes more. If any of the mussels or cockles don't open when most of the others have, discard them; if any clams haven't opened, stick a knife in between the two shells and give it a little twist—most of the time they just pop open and are fine, but give a sniff just to be sure. Arrange the seafood in 4 heated bowls and pour the liquid into a small saucepan, leaving any grit behind.

3. Bring the liquid to a simmer and add the scallops; poach for 1 minute. Add the oysters and turn off the heat—you just want to warm them through. Arrange the additional seafood in the bowls. Add the herbs and cream to the liquid, bring to a simmer, and whisk in the butter, one tablespoon at a time; keep whisking until all the butter is combined. Season with salt, keeping in mind that the sauce will already be salty, and pepper. Ladle the sauce into the bowls and serve.

Lobster and Shrimp Ragout

MAKES: 4 main course servings

This is a great dish if you want the flavor of lobster but the crunchy texture and less expensive abundance of shrimp. The trick is to extract the flavor from the lobster—and this dish tastes more like lobster than lobster itself—and use it as a sauce for shrimp with just a little bit of lobster. It only requires one lobster for four servings. This dish is somewhat labor-intensive but much of the work can be done early on the day you serve. One last detail: The lobster has to be cut up alive.

EARLIER ON THE DAY OF SERVING

1. Rinse off the lobster and kill it by placing it on a cutting board and, holding the knife vertically straight above the lobster's "head," push the knife all the way through to the board. Bend the knife forward so the front half of the head is cut in half—this kills the lobster humanely. Hold the lobster over a bowl containing the vinegar (the vinegar keeps the juices from congealing) to catch any juices that run out after you cut into the lobster. Place a strainer over the bowl. Twist the tail away from the head—actually the thorax—and use your fingers to reach into the thorax and tail to pull out any dark green roe and pale green tomalley. Let the roe and tomalley fall into the strainer. Use a wooden spoon or your fingers to work the roe and tomalley through the strainer. Refrigerate the mixture in the bowl. Twist the claws away from the thorax. Slide a small skewer along the outer membrane that runs along the inside of the tail to prevent the tail from curling while cooking.

2. In a large sauté pan, heat the oil over high heat until it ripples and add the lobster parts. Stir them around until they're bright red on all sides, about 5 minutes, and turn the heat down to medium. Take out the lobster pieces and add the onion to the pan. Stir for about 5 minutes and add the tomatoes, the tarragon, and the thyme. Put the lobster pieces back in and simmer gently, covered, for 10 minutes. 7 minutes into the cooking, add the shrimp and cook, along with the lobster, for 3 minutes. Take the lobster pieces and shrimp out of the pan and let cool. Take the pan off the heat.

1 lobster (ask for female)

1 teaspoon white wine vinegar

3 tablespoons olive oil

1 small onion, chopped fine

4 tomatoes, stemmed and chopped coarse

4 sprigs fresh tarragon

3 sprigs fresh or dried thyme

12 jumbo shrimp, preferably with heads, peeled, deveined (deveining optional), shells and heads reserved

salt and pepper to taste

4 chervil sprigs (optional)

3. Take the meat out of the lobster and reserve. Put the shell from the lobster tail (not the claws, which would damage the food processor) and the shrimp shells and heads into a food processor and chop for 1 minute. Put this mixture into the pan with the tomatoes and simmer gently for 10 minutes. Work the mixture in the pan through a strainer into a small saucepan and reserve. Cut the lobster tail into 4 equal slices. Cut each of the claws in half lengthwise so you have 4 halves.

JUST BEFORE SERVING

1. Put the lobster pieces and the shrimp on a heatproof plate and cover tightly with aluminum foil. Place the covered plate in an oven on its very lowest setting.

2. Bring the tomato mixture in the saucepan to a simmer, then whisk it into the chilled coral mixture. Transfer the tomato-roe/tomalley mixture back into the saucepan and whisk continuously over very low heat. If the lobster contained dark green roe, the sauce will gradually turn from a dull green to a bright orange. Season to taste with salt and pepper. Arrange the lobster pieces and shrimp in hot soup plates and spoon the sauce over them. Decorate each with a sprig of chervil, if desired.

Shrimp Vindaloo

MAKES: 4 main course servings

One doesn't actually see shrimp vindaloo on Indian menus since the tra-ditional dish is made with pork, and derivatives seem to be limited to chicken and lamb. But the treatment works amazingly well with shrimp, especially if the shrimp is brined first to give it the necessary contrasting crunch. The secret to this recipe is a mountain of garlic, a special spice mixture, and a combination of vinegar and sugar whose opposing tastes amplify all the other components. The chiles here, while not the chiles used in India, are all smoked and give the dish an extra note of complexity. Pasilla de Oaxaca chiles can be hard to find but their rich smokiness makes them worth the effort.

1. In a small sauté pan, heat the spices, except the pepper and ginger, in a tablespoon of ghee over low to medium heat until fragrant, about 2 minutes. Take off the heat and stir in the pepper, ginger, chiles, vinegar, and garlic.

2. Cook the onion slices over medium heat in a sauté pan in the remain-ing ghee until translucent and then pale brown, about 15 minutes. Add the tomatoes. Simmer gently, stirring every couple of minutes to prevent sticking, until the mixture thickens, about 15 minutes. Add the sugar, more vinegar if needed, and season to taste with salt. Just before serving, add the shrimp to the hot tomato mixture and simmer for 3 minutes. Serve with basmati rice.

¼ teaspoon ground cardamom

¼ teaspoon ground cinnamon

⅛ teaspoon ground cloves

½ teaspoon fresh ground pepper

½ teaspoon ground cumin

½ teaspoon ground coriander

2 teaspoons paprika

1 teaspoon ground turmeric

3 tablespoons ghee (see page 94), butter, or vegetable oil

1 teaspoon freshly ground black pepper

one 1-inch piece fresh ginger, peeled and grated fine

2 dried chipotle or Pasilla de Oaxaca chiles, soaked for 30 minutes in warm water and drained, or 2 canned chipo-tle chiles in adobo sauce, sauce rinsed off, or 4 jalapeño chiles, stemmed, seeded, and chopped fine

¼ cup sherry vinegar, excellent quality balsamic vinegar, or ½ cup inexpen-sive balsamic vinegar boiled down to ¼ cup, or more to taste

6 cloves garlic, minced and crushed to a paste with the side of a chef's knife

2 large red onions, sliced very fine

6 medium tomatoes, peeled (see page 21), seeded, and chopped fine

2 teaspoons sugar

salt

20 jumbo shrimp, peeled and deveined (deveining optional)

Steamed or boiled basmati rice (for serving)

Shrimp "Mouclade"

MAKES: 8 hors d'oeuvre or first course servings or 4 main course servings

A mouclade differs from other French fish stews and soups in that it contains curry. This dish is a misnomer since the original mouclade *from Brittany gets its name from mussels. In this recipe, the juices released by mussels serve as a light, broth-like sauce for shrimp. You can serve this dish as a soup with the shrimp floating in the broth or you can just serve it in a big bowl in the center of the table and let people reach for the shrimp until they get to the best part: the creamy juices in the bottom of the bowl.*

1. Scrub the mussels. While you're scrubbing, push the shells sideways in opposing directions so any dead mussels will fall apart in your hand. If the mussels are gaping it doesn't necessarily mean they are bad—tap them together and they should slowly close. If still uncertain, give a sniff—a bad mussel leaves no doubt.

2. Combine the wine and garlic in a pot large enough to hold the mussels and bring to a gentle simmer. Add the mussels, cover the pot, and simmer until all the mussels open, about 5 minutes. If one or two of the mussels don't open, remove them very carefully from the pot and discard. Take the mussels out of the shells and if the beards are big, pull them off and discard them. Keep the mussels warm while you cook the shrimp.

3. Put the shrimp in the pot with the mussel cooking liquid, cover the pot, and steam over medium heat for 3 to 4 minutes, until all the shrimp are bright red. While the shrimp are cooking, cook the curry powder and turmeric in the butter in a small sauté pan over medium heat until the curry is fragrant, 1–2 minutes. Take the shrimp out of the pot with a skimmer and keep them warm in a serving bowl. If there's grit in the pot, gently pour the liquid into a saucepan, leaving any grit behind. Add the chives and parsley to the liquid, then the curry mixture and the cream. Grind in some pepper. Simmer for 2 minutes. Add the mussels to the serving bowl containing the shrimp, combine, and pour the liquid over them. Serve with plenty of crunchy baguette for dipping.

2 pounds mussels

⅔ cup dry white wine, preferably somewhat acidic like a Muscadet or Sauvignon Blanc or something from the Loire valley, or dry sherry, such as fino or dry oloroso

1 clove garlic, minced and crushed to a paste with the side of a chef's knife

40 large or 32 jumbo shrimp

1 tablespoon curry powder

2 tablespoons ground turmeric

2 tablespoons butter

1 medium bunch chives, chopped very fine (optional)

1 medium bunch parsley, large stems removed, leaves and small stems chopped just before using

1 cup heavy cream

pepper to taste

Shrimp with Garlic Sauce

MAKES: 6 first course servings

2 heads garlic

½ cup heavy cream, half-and-half, or milk

7 fresh sage leaves, 1 chopped fine

½ small bunch parsley, large stems removed, leaves and small stems chopped very fine

salt and pepper to taste

12 large or 6 jumbo shrimp, peeled and deveined (deveining optional)

The inspiration for this recipe is a French dish for frogs' legs with a sauce made from garlic purée. The garlic is blanched thoroughly before it's puréed into the sauce, a treatment that makes it surprisingly subtle. Oddly, though, be prepared to smell garlic for at least 12 hours after eating this dish. If you can find it, use fresh spring garlic. Usually sauces cannot be made with milk or half-and-half unless they contain flour to prevent them from curdling, but here, the garlic purée will prevent curdling. The sauce can be made early on the day of serving.

1. Break up the garlic heads and soak the cloves for 5 minutes in warm water to make them easier to peel. Peel the cloves without crushing them. Put the garlic in a saucepan with about 4 quarts of water and boil for 25 minutes. Drain and discard the cooking water. Reserve 12 to 18 of the smallest cloves and put 12 of the largest cloves back in the saucepan with the cream, the sage leaves, and the chopped sage and bring to a simmer. Remove from the heat and let sit for 15 minutes to infuse the sage, but don't let the mixture get cold or, if you're using cream, the cream will break when you beat it. Take out the whole sage leaves and reserve. Purée this mixture with an immersion blender, regular blender, or by working it through a strainer with a wooden spoon. Combine with the parsley and season to taste with salt and pepper.

2. When you're ready to serve, put the shrimp and the reserved garlic cloves in the sauce and bring to a simmer over medium heat. Stir the shrimp over low to medium heat for about 4 minutes. If the sauce gets too thick, thin it with a little cream or water. Make a small pool of sauce in the center of 6 heated plates and place a 2 large shrimp or 1 jumbo shrimp on each one. Decorate with the sage leaves and small garlic cloves. (Heat the garlic in the microwave if it's gotten cold.)

sautéed and fried shrimp

Basic Sautéed Shrimp

MAKES: 6 main course servings

30 large or 24 jumbo shrimp,
   peeled and deveined (peeling and
   deveining optional)

2 tablespoons olive oil or butter

salt and pepper to taste

Perhaps the easiest and most versatile way to cook shrimp, sautéing only requires a pan and a little oil or butter. Shrimp that's sautéed in its shell will retain its flavor better than shrimp that's been shelled. But you may not want to force your guests to peel their own shrimp—even though in Europe, especially in Italy where they adore the shellfish, shrimp always arrives at the table still in its head and shells. There are times, however, when you have to sauté the shrimp out of its shell: If you're sautéing it with a flavorful ingredient that you want to permeate the shrimp, it's better to peel the shrimp before cooking.

Rinse off the shrimp and heat the oil or butter in a sauté pan or wok over high heat. When the oil begins to ripple or the butter is frothy, add the shrimp all at once. Toss the shrimp by pulling the pan toward you with a sudden jerk—this gets the shrimp to "jump" out of the pan (*sauter* means "to jump" in French)—in the way of professional cooks, or stir the shrimp with a pair of chopsticks or a wooden spoon. When the shrimp are all bright red, in 3 to 4 minutes, season with salt and pepper to taste and serve immediately.

Sautéed Shrimp with Parsley and Garlic

MAKES: 6 main course servings

Anyone who likes snails soon realizes that it's the pungent parsley and garlic butter served with them that provides all the flavor; snails themselves hardly taste like anything at all. While shrimp sautéed in the shell retains more of its own flavor, you can also sauté the shrimp out of the shell so the flavors permeate it. An extra bonus is that all the parsley-garlic flavor is trapped in the butter and released all at once in the hot sauté pan, flavoring the shrimp and filling the kitchen with a delightful aroma.

¾ cup (1 ½ sticks) unsalted butter

1 medium bunch parsley, preferably Italian flat leaf, large stems removed, chopped very fine just before using

2 cloves garlic, minced and crushed to a paste with the side of a chef's knife

2 tablespoons olive oil

36 large or 24 jumbo shrimp (deveining optional)

1. Slice the butter into thin slices. Add the parsley and continue chopping the butter. This seals in the flavor of the parsley. Chop in the garlic. Reserve, wrapped in plastic, in the fridge, until you're ready to sauté.

2. Heat the olive oil in a sauté pan or wok over high heat. When it starts to ripple, add all the shrimp at once, and stir or toss for 1 minute. Add the parsley-garlic butter all at once and continue stirring around the shrimp for another 2 minutes. At this point the butter should be frothy and completely coat the shrimp. Serve on hot plates with plenty of bread for soaking up the butter.

VARIATIONS: The idea of mixing flavorful ingredients with butter is nothing new. Flavored butters, called compound butters, have been around for centuries. One advantage to a compound butter is that you can prepare it in advance without it losing its flavor as would most chopped herbs on their own. So feel free to invent your own compound butters—some favorites are included on the next page.

FRESH MARJORAM BUTTER: Chop 3 tablespoons fresh marjoram leaves coarse and combine them with ½ cup (1 stick) butter. Chop the butter until the marjoram is chopped fine. If you like, mince and crush a clove of garlic and work it into the butter.

TARRAGON BUTTER: Coarsely chop ¼ cup fresh tarragon leaves and combine with ½ cup (1 stick) butter. Chop the butter until the tarragon is chopped fine.

CHERVIL BUTTER: Replace the tarragon in the recipe above with chervil.

Improvising Sauces for Sautéed Shrimp

When you sauté shrimp and add a compound butter, you end up with a sauce of sorts—a pungent, flavorful butter. But because melted butter is oily and not really sauce-like, some cooks like to make a pan-deglazed sauce that will stay smooth and emulsified and can be served over or under the shrimp. The possibilities for improvising these kinds of sauces seem to be limitless, but they all follow a basic formula: The hot shrimp is taken out of the pan—ideally it's been sautéed in the shell and you have an assistant who can peel it while you make the sauce—and the fat is wiped out of the sauté pan. The pan is then "deglazed" with a flavorful liquid such as white wine, Madeira, port, or sherry; broth or reduced broth is added; some kind of emulsifier such as cream or butter is stirred in; and the sauce is finished with herbs or maybe a few drops of certain spirits. Because shrimp don't really leave any juices in the sauté pan with which to deglaze, there's no point in constructing a pan-deglazed sauce at the very last minute—it's easiest just to make it in a saucepan up to an hour before serving.

Shrimp with Tomatoes and Tarragon

MAKES: 6 main course servings

4 ripe tomatoes, chopped

½ cup dry sherry

⅓ cup cognac

½ cup heavy cream

1 recipe Tarragon Butter (see page 115)

1 tablespoon good quality white wine vinegar or more as needed

salt and pepper to taste

30 large shrimp, peeled and deveined (peeling and deveining optional)

While this sauce takes a little work, most of the work—making the tarragon butter and the tomato purée—can be done up to 3 days in advance. The cognac is optional, but if you do decide to include it, use a genuine cognac (the real thing has the word "cognac" on the bottle) not a generic brandy, which won't have any flavor. On the other hand, buy the least expensive cognac you can find—the finesse of a finer cognac will be lost during cooking.

1. Put the tomatoes in a heavy-bottomed saucepan over low to medium heat. Cover the pan and simmer for 15 minutes, checking and stirring every couple of minutes to make sure the tomatoes don't stick to the bottom of the saucepan and scald. Work the tomatoes through a food mill or strainer and then through a fine-mesh strainer if you have one. Reserve this purée for up to 3 days in the refrigerator.

2. Within an hour of serving, boil the sherry down by half in a small saucepan. Add the cognac and boil down by half. Add the tomato purée and the cream and simmer over medium heat until the sauce has the consistency you like—usually it's best when it just coats the back of a spoon. Cut the Tarragon Butter into 4 pieces and add them all at once to the sauce. Immediately stir in the butter pieces with a whisk. Don't stop whisking until all the butter is incorporated or it will turn oily. Add the vinegar to taste and season to taste with salt and pepper.

3. Depending on the consistency of the sauce, use it to line the bottom of heated plates or soup bowls and arrange the shrimp on top. Add the peeled shrimp to the sauce and simmer for 3 to 4 minutes.

Shrimp Teriyaki

MAKES: 6 main course servings

A simple teriyaki glaze is a perfect accent to sautéed or grilled shrimp. While some recipes are more complex than this one, most teriyaki glazes are made with sake, mirin, and soy sauce. Mirin is a kind of syrupy sweet wine that's a staple of Japanese cooking, but sugar is a perfect substitute that some people, in fact, prefer. Just make sure you buy an authentic Japanese soy sauce—Kikkoman is a good brand and easy to find. The shrimp for this recipe must be peeled so they get coated with the sauce.

⅔ cup soy sauce

¼ cup sugar

36 large or 24 jumbo shrimp, peeled and deveined (deveining optional)

2 tablespoons olive oil or vegetable oil

sesame seeds, toasted for about 15 minutes in a 350°F oven

1. Heat the soy sauce in a small saucepan and add the sugar; stir until it completely dissolves.

2. Rinse off the shrimp and heat the oil in a sauté pan or wok over high heat. When the oil begins to ripple, add the shrimp all at once. Toss the shrimp by pulling the pan toward you with a sudden jerk—this gets the shrimp to "jump" out of the pan, or stir the shrimp with a pair of chopsticks or a wooden spoon. When the shrimp just begin to turn red, in 3 to 4 minutes, take them out of the pan with a spider utensil or skimmer and reserve on a plate. Wipe any oil out of the pan with a paper towel and pour in the soy sauce–sugar mixture. Bring to a boil over high heat and when the sauce is reduced by about half, put the shrimp back in. Sprinkle the sesame seeds over the shrimp and stir the shrimp around in the sauce, still over high heat, until they're well coated with a shiny glaze, about 2 minutes. Serve immediately.

Shrimp Cakes

MAKES: 8 first course or 4 main course servings (8 shrimp cakes)

1 ½ pounds shrimp of any size, peeled and deveined

4 slices dense-crumb white sandwich bread, crusts removed

⅓ cup milk or reduced Creamy Shrimp Broth (see page 68)

1 egg, beaten

2 teaspoons curry powder

6 tablespoons butter

1 medium bunch parsley, large stems removed, leaves and small stems chopped fine just before using

salt to taste

1 cup Saffron Aioli (see page 179), Caper and Herb Mayonnaise (see page 178), or 2 cups Tropical Fruit Salsa (see page 172)

An obvious derivative of crab cakes, shrimp cakes are especially tasty when served with Saffron Aioli or Caper and Herb Mayonnaise. If you want something lighter, try some Tropical Fruit Salsa. These cakes contain curry powder, which you are free to leave out. You can chop the shrimp by hand, but it's better to use a food processor; use the pulse mechanism and go about it slowly so you don't turn the shrimp into a dense paste. Work the milk-soaked bread in by hand—mix just enough to incorporate it. If you want to give the cakes a deeper flavor, reduce 1 cup of Creamy Shrimp Broth down to ¼ cup and use it instead of the milk to soak the breadcrumbs.

1. Chop the shrimp to the texture of coarse meal in a food processor.

2. Soak the bread in the milk and the egg. Cook the curry powder in 2 tablespoons of the butter in a small sauté pan over low to medium heat until fragrant, about 30 seconds. Add this to the egg mixture along with the chopped parsley. Transfer the egg mixture to the food processor, and process the shrimp and egg mixtures just long enough to mix them well—don't overwork the mixture. Season to taste with salt. If you're squeamish about tasting raw shrimp, fry up a tiny piece for tasting.

3. Shape the mixture into patties—you'll need about ⅓ cup per patty— about 3 inches across or, if you want to make smaller cakes, use ¼ cup of mixture to make 2 ¼-inch patties. Just before you're ready to serve, sauté the cakes, over medium heat, in the remaining butter, for about 4 minutes on each side. Serve immediately with one of the sauces.

Stir-fried Shrimp with Orange and Julienned Vegetables

MAKES: 6 main course servings

¼ pound snow peas, ends snapped off and peas julienned about ¹/₁₆-inch thick

4 medium shiitake mushrooms, stems removed and caps julienned about ¹/₁₆-inch thick

1 large carrot, peeled and julienned

1 red or green bell pepper, stemmed, seeded, and julienned

1 serrano or jalapeño chile, stemmed, halved, seeded, and julienned as fine as possible

1 small celeriac, peeled, sliced as fine as possible, and julienned (optional)

1 medium red onion, sliced very fine

1 orange

2 tablespoons peanut oil

one 1-inch piece fresh ginger, peeled and grated fine

1 clove garlic, minced and crushed to a paste with the side of a chef's knife

2 teaspoons sugar

1 tablespoon balsamic vinegar, or more to taste

2 tablespoons soy sauce

1 teaspoon cornstarch (optional)

30 large shrimp, peeled and deveined (deveining optional)

The trick to successful stir-frying is to cut the vegetables small enough so they cook quickly and retain their crunch and color. In this recipe you can add or eliminate whatever vegetables you wish. The inclusion of orange is inspired by the traditional Chinese restaurant dish Beef with Orange, but it works amazingly well with shrimp, especially when you add vinegar to create a sweet-and-sour effect.

1. When you've julienned all the vegetables and sliced the onion, trim off two 3-inch strips of zest from the orange. Slice into fine julienne. Squeeze the orange and reserve the juice.

2. In a wok or large sauté pan, heat the peanut oil over medium heat and add the ginger and garlic. Stir until they sizzle a few seconds, turn the heat to high, and add the vegetables. Stir-fry the vegetables for about 5 minutes. Combine the sugar, vinegar, orange juice, soy sauce, and cornstarch, if using, in a small bowl. Add the orange zest, shrimp, and sugar-vinegar mixture to the vegetables and stir until the shrimp are bright red, about 4 minutes. Serve on heated plates.

Fried Shrimp with Crispy Batter

MAKES: 36 shrimp

The trick to successful frying is to get the food as quickly as possible from the hot oil to the diner's mouth. Fried food that sits on a plate, for even a minute, loses some of the bright flavor and excitement that makes frying worth the calories and the dangers of cooking with hot oil.

Apart from immersing peeled shrimp directly in hot oil, the only available variations of fried shrimp come from using different batters. The simplest batter, a light mixture of flour and water with the consistency of heavy cream, works as well as any even though there are those who insist on including beer, eggs, or soda water. One trick that does work is to include yeast in a flour and water batter and then let the batter sit in a warm place for an hour or two. The yeast produces carbon dioxide that lightens the batter and gives it a pleasant fermented flavor.

These shrimp are best served as an hors d'oeuvre.

1 ½ cups warm (not hot) water

1 cup all-purpose flour

1 teaspoon active dry yeast, dissolved for 10 minutes in warm water

2 quarts vegetable oil

36 large or extra large shrimp, peeled except for the tail and deveined (deveining optional)

salt to taste

assorted mayonnaises and/or chutneys (see pages 174, 176–79, and 180)

1. Whisk the water into the flour in a small mixing bowl. As soon as the batter is smooth—don't worry about a few lumps—stop whisking so you don't overwork the batter and make it tough. Stir in the yeast and its soaking liquid, cover the batter with plastic wrap, and let it sit in a warm place for 1 to 2 hours or until doubled in volume (exact timing depends on the temperature of your kitchen).

2. Heat the oil in a heavy pot large enough so that the oil doesn't come higher than halfway up the sides. If you have a frying thermometer, heat the oil to 370°F. If you don't have a thermometer, drop a dollop of batter into the oil. When the batter rises, surrounded with bubbles, within 5 seconds, the oil is ready. Start slowly—a couple of shrimp at a time—until you get a sense of how the oil is behaving. Ideally, the shrimp should take about 1 minute to brown—this ensures that they are cooked through (which they won't be if the oil is too hot). If the oil isn't hot enough, the batter will be soggy.

3. Fry the shrimp, about 6 at a time, drain on paper towels, sprinkle liberally with salt, and serve immediately with the mayonnaises and/or chutneys, if desired.

dumplings, pasta, risotto, and more

Shrimp Dumplings with Dried Chile Sauce

MAKES: 48 dumplings (8 servings of 6 dumplings each)

The idea for this dish comes from Susanna Foo's insightful book Chinese Cuisine. *She uses pork, but the basic flavor combinations are similar. Any of the more common Mexican dried chiles can be used for this dish, but anchos, guajillos, and mulatos are the easiest to find and aren't too hot.*

FOR THE SAUCE

1 medium onion, chopped fine

2 jalapeño chiles, seeded and chopped fine

1 tablespoon Szechwan peppercorns

2 tablespoons vegetable oil

3 dried ancho or guajillo chiles, soaked in warm water for 30 minutes and drained, stemmed, seeded, and chopped fine

½ cup dry fino sherry, such as Dry Sack, or Noilly Prat vermouth

3 star anise

1¾ cups brown chicken broth

salt to taste

MAKING THE SAUCE

In a medium saucepan, cook the onion, jalapeño chiles, and Szechwan peppercorns in the vegetable oil for about 10 minutes over medium heat—long enough for the onion to turn pale brown. Stir often so the onions brown evenly. Add the chiles to the onion mixture, stirring over medium heat for about 2 minutes more, then add the sherry. Turn the heat up to high and boil the mixture for about 1 minute to cook off the alcohol in the sherry. Crush the star anise under a saucepan and add it to the onion mixture. Cook over medium heat for 1 minute. Put the onion-chile mixture in a blender and pour the warm (but not hot) chicken broth through the top, a little at a time, until you've added enough to get the mixture to move around in the blender. Purée for about a minute and add the rest of the broth. Season to taste with salt. Pour the mixture through a strainer set over a bowl or saucepan. You can keep this sauce for up to a week in the refrigerator, tightly covered.

MAKING THE DUMPLING FILLING

In a food processor, combine the bacon, shrimp, scallions, garlic, ginger, soy sauce, and sesame oil and purée for 30 seconds. Scrape down the sides with a rubber spatula and purée 30 seconds more. Transfer to a mixing bowl. Soak the bread in the milk for 5 minutes and work it with your fingers until you have a wet paste; stir this into the shrimp mixture. Reserve, covered with plastic wrap, in the refrigerator.

FOR THE DUMPLINGS

¼ pound good quality smoky bacon, strips cut crosswise into smaller strips

¾ pound headless shrimp, peeled and deveined (deveining optional)

6 scallions, white part and 3 inches of green part, sliced thin

1 medium clove garlic, minced and crushed to a paste with the side of a chef's knife

one 1-inch piece fresh ginger, peeled and grated fine

2 tablespoons Japanese soy sauce

1 tablespoon Japanese dark sesame oil

3 slices white bread, crusts removed

1 cup milk

one 14-ounce package 4-inch-round wonton wrappers (60 wrappers)

MAKING THE DUMPLINGS

1. When working with wonton wrappers, keep them tightly wrapped when not in use to prevent them from drying out.

2. Place 1 ½ teaspoons of the shrimp mixture in the center of each wrapper. Brush around the mound with water and bring the sides of the circle up around the mound and pinch together. At this point you can place the dumplings on a sheet pan and freeze them.

FINISHING AND SERVING

1. Bring 6 quarts of water to a boil and add the dumplings. As soon as you add the dumplings the water will stop boiling. Allow it to come back to a very gentle simmer but then turn down the heat to keep the water from boiling—if it boils the dumplings may burst open. Simmer for 5 minutes and drain in a colander or remove with a spider utensil.

2. While the dumplings are simmering, bring the sauce to a simmer.

3. Use a small pitcher to pour 3 to 4 tablespoons of the sauce into 8 wide soup plates and arrange 6 dumplings on top of each plate.

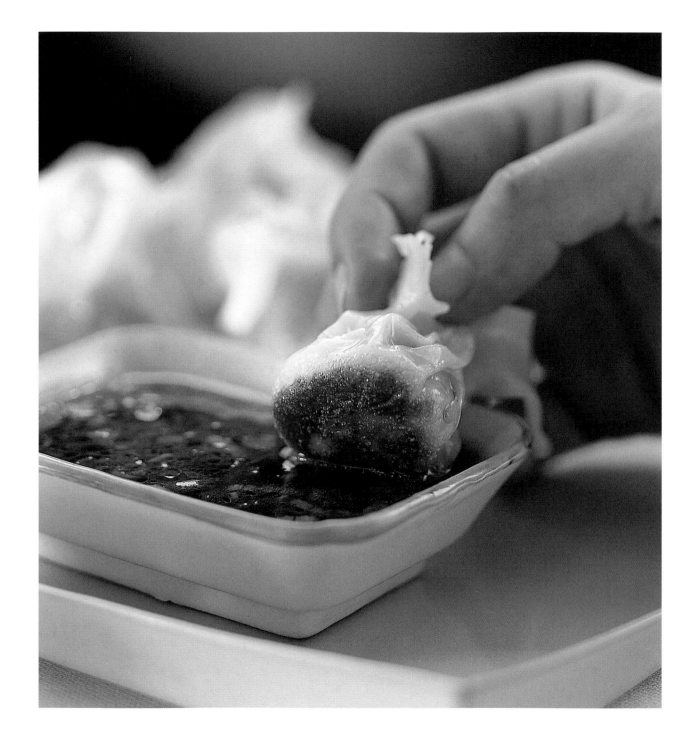

Pot Stickers

These are essentially shrimp dumplings that are browned on the bottom in a nonstick pan instead of being poached. They are then served with a savory dipping sauce that makes them a perfect passed-around hors d'oeuvre or first course.

1. Combine all the sauce ingredients and let sit in the refrigerator for an hour or longer. (The sauce will keep for at least a week, tightly covered.)

2. Bring about 6 quarts of water to a boil, add the dumplings, and regulate the heat to maintain a gentle simmer for 5 minutes. Remove the dumplings with a slotted spoon or spider utensil onto a flat surface (not paper towels, which will stick). Working in batches of 24 or more—depending on the size of your pans—heat 2 tablespoons of the oil over medium heat in a nonstick sauté pan. Heat the dumplings over medium heat until golden brown on the bottom, 2 to 3 minutes if the dumplings just came out of the water, or 5 to 6 minutes if the dumplings started out cold. Serve with the dipping sauce.

FOR THE DIPPING SAUCE

3 tablespoons Japanese soy sauce

3 tablespoons plus 2 teaspoons rice wine vinegar or white wine vinegar

2 tablespoons mirin

1 tablespoon plus 1 teaspoon sesame oil

1 clove garlic, minced and crushed to a paste with the side of a chef's knife

one 1-inch piece fresh ginger, peeled and grated fine (about 1 tablespoon)

1 scallion, white and light green parts sliced very fine

1 recipe Shrimp Dumplings (see page 125)

about 6 tablespoons peanut oil or vegetable oil

Fettuccini with Shrimp Sauce

MAKES: 4 main course or 6 first course servings

1 quart Creamy Shrimp Broth
    (see page 68)

¼ cup heavy cream (optional)

½ teaspoon saffron threads, soaked for
    30 minutes in 1 tablespoon water
    (optional)

1 pound medium shrimp, shelled and
    deveined (deveining optional)

1 pound fresh fettuccini or 12 ounces
    dried fettucini

The Italian dish fettuccini à la crema di scampi *is essentially the same as this one except that it's made with scampi instead of shrimp (scampi look a bit like miniature lobsters; they're known in France as* langoustines) *but the treatment and resulting flavor is much the same. In Rome the dish is served with none of the actual shellfish—just the sauce made from the shells. It's up to you to include shrimp as part of the dish, but it's probably a good idea if you're serving this dish as a main course. Making the sauce is a simple matter of boiling down the Creamy Shrimp Broth.*

1. Put the broth in a large saucepan and bring to a simmer. Simmer for about 15 minutes, until it cooks down to about one-third to one-quarter of its original volume and has the consistency you like—usually best when it just coats the back of a spoon. Beat it with a whisk every few minutes as it's simmering to keep it from separating. Whisk in the cream and the saffron and its soaking liquid, if using, and simmer again to the consistency you like. When the water's ready for the pasta, bring the sauce to a simmer and stir in the shrimp. (If you are using dried fettuccine, wait to add the shrimp until the last 3 minutes of cooking.)

2. Bring a large pot of water to a boil for the pasta and boil according to the directions on the package or 2 to 4 minutes for fresh fettuccini and 7 minutes for dried. Bite into a piece to see if it's ready—it should be al dente—and drain in a colander. Return the pasta to the pot and pour in the sauce. Toss the pasta with the sauce and serve on hot plates.

Shrimp Risotto

MAKES: 4 to 6 first course servings

The subject of risotto never fails to create arguments among Italophiles. Most have to do with what kind of rice to use—carnaroli, Arborio, and violone nano are the usual contestants—but there are often disputes about the correct consistency as well. Italians seem to use the rice that's from their particular region: In Venice, risotto is on the soupy side—they call it l'onda (like a wave)—whereas in Milan it's rather stiff. The choice of consistency is yours but try it on the wet side if you've never had it that way—it's somehow lighter. Many American cooks serve risotto as a side dish as they might a pilaf or plain cooked rice, but risotto is meant to be a bit more special than that and makes a lovely first course. Many people hesitate to make risotto for guests because of the need for almost 20 minutes of constant stirring. The solution is to cook the risotto for about 10 minutes ahead of time and then finish it just before serving.

Bring the shrimp broth and the chicken broth to a gentle simmer in separate saucepans. In a large saucepan, cook the onion and garlic in the 2 tablespoons olive oil over medium heat, stirring every minute or so, until the onion turns translucent but doesn't brown, about 8 minutes. Add the rice and stir over medium heat for about 2 minutes. Add a cup of the shrimp broth and stir for 1 minute, or until the broth disappears. Add another cup and stir again; continue in this way until you've used all the shrimp broth, and then start using the chicken broth. After 15 minutes, start nibbling on a grain of rice to check for doneness—there should be just the slightest resistance—and add only ½ cup of liquid at a time so you don't add too much and make the rice too runny. The consistency can range from almost as stiff as a pilaf to the consistency of loose baked beans, but you should keep the risotto slightly on the stiff side because when you add the butter and olive oil it's going to get runnier. When the rice is done, usually after about 25 minutes, stir in the saffron, remaining olive oil, butter, and shrimp. If the risotto is too stiff, add just enough hot broth or water to give it the consistency you like. Season to taste with salt and pepper. Serve on hot plates or soup plates.

1 quart Creamy Shrimp Broth (page 68)

1 quart chicken broth or water

1 medium white or yellow onion, chopped fine

1 clove garlic, minced

¼ cup plus 2 tablespoons extra virgin olive oil

2 cups (8 ounces) unrinsed short-grain rice such as *carnaroli*, Arborio, or *violone nano*

½ teaspoon saffron threads, soaked for 30 minutes in 1 tablespoon water (optional)

½ cup (1 stick) unsalted butter

18 large shrimp, peeled, deveined, and cut into ⅓-inch dice (optional)

salt and pepper to taste

Shrimp Ravioli

MAKES: 48 small ravioli (6 first course servings or 4 main course servings)

When most people cook elaborate ravioli, they make the mistake of surrounding them with a sauce that tastes a lot like the filling. A better approach is to serve the ravioli in a simple broth that's neither too rich nor too flavorful, so that when you bite into the ravioli the flavor of the filling bursts out in contrast. Another mistake is making the filling too dry or too thick—it should liquefy as the ravioli cook so that when you bite into one it fills your mouth with flavor. To pull this off, the filling has to contain a fair amount of fat that's solid when you're making the ravioli but liquefies once hot. It should be stated that these ravioli are rich, since they are essentially made with shrimp puréed in a food processor with butter, or even better, shrimp butter. They can be made lighter by including less butter, but then the liquid bursting effect will be lost. A simple chicken broth serves as a neutral foil. The ravioli should be made small so diners can eat them whole (if they cut into them the filling will leak out) and should be served only with spoons so no one tries to spear them with a fork. These ravioli should be cooked the same day they're made or the pasta will start to look dark—although the flavor is fine for 2 days.

PREPARING THE DOUGH

Combine the flour, eggs, and salt in a food processor and process until the mixture comes together in a shaggy mass, about 30 seconds. Dump the dough out onto the work surface and knead it, sprinkling flour over it as needed, until it's smooth and no longer sticky, about 5 minutes. Wrap the dough in plastic and let it rest for 10 minutes or longer. Cut it into 3 pieces. Stretch each of the pieces, fold it in half, and work each piece through a pasta machine at the thickest setting; if the dough sticks, sprinkle it with flour. Fold it in half and stretch, work through again, fold, work through, and continue in this way for about 3 minutes for each piece until the dough doesn't tear at all in the machine and takes on the texture of soft suede. If the dough is tearing or hard to work through the machine you may be not stretching it enough before you put it into the machine and it may be too thick. When all the dough is kneaded, set the machine to the next thinnest setting and roll the 3 pieces through. Set to

FOR THE DOUGH

3¾ cups all-purpose flour, plus more for kneading

6 eggs

½ teaspoon salt

FOR THE FILLING

9 ounces shell-on shrimp or 7 ounces peeled shrimp of any size

½ cup (1 stick) plus 2 tablespoons unsalted butter

1 tablespoon fresh marjoram or tarragon leaves, chopped just before using

1¼ teaspoons salt

½ teaspoon pepper

FOR THE BROTH

2 cups chicken broth

the next setting and roll again; continue until you've rolled all the dough through the second to the thinnest setting—machines vary but most make pasta too thin at the thinnest setting. As you're rolling the dough, the sheets will become awkwardly long: Cut them crosswise in half, making sure the halves are the same length, so you end up with 6 sheets, each about 24 inches long and 5 inches wide. If you're not using the sheets right away, place them on wax paper–lined sheet pans and cover them with plastic wrap so they don't dry out.

PREPARING THE FILLING

Combine the shrimp, butter, marjoram, salt, and pepper in a food processor and process for 2 minutes. Scrape down the sides once or twice to make sure everything is well puréed. Refrigerate until needed.

ASSEMBLING THE RAVIOLI

A: Spread out one of the sheets of dough and arrange the filling in 2 rows of 8 mounds each, using about 1 ½ teaspoons of filling per mound. **B and C:** Brush around the filling with water and arrange another sheet of dough over the mounds. **D, E, and F:** Press all around the ravioli to seal them and do your best to press out any air pockets that have formed next to the mounds. **G and H:** Cut out the ravioli with a square or round fluted 2½-inch cookie cutter and place them on a wax paper–lined sheet pan to prevent sticking.

SIMMERING AND SERVING

Bring about 8 quarts of water to a boil and bring the broth to a simmer in a separate saucepan. Add the ravioli all at once to the water and wait for it to return to a simmer. At that point turn down the heat to a bare simmer—if the water boils the ravioli can burst open—and simmer for about 5 minutes. Drain in a colander and very carefully spoon the ravioli into hot soup bowls—8 each for first courses, 12 each for main courses. Ladle the hot broth over each serving, ⅓ cup for first course servings and ½ cup for main course servings.

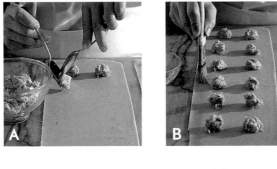

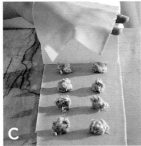

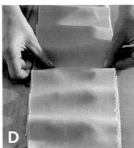

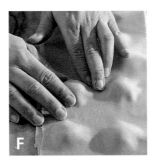

Summer Rolls

MAKES: 25 summer rolls (50 halves),
enough to serve 12 as hors d'oeuvres or a first course

Fresh summer rolls made at the last minute are a delight, a cool and crunchy hors d'oeuvre or even a first course. The concept is simple: wrapping seafood or meat and some crunchy vegetables in rice paper with a strong salty and tart sauce that makes the flavors sing. Don't confuse the rice-paper rounds used for making spring rolls with egg roll or wonton wrappers, and be sure to make the dipping sauce before embarking on the summer rolls so the sauce flavors have time to infuse.

PREPARING THE DIPPING SAUCE

1. Combine all the sauce ingredients, and stir until the sugar dissolves. Add more sugar or fish sauce to taste.

ASSEMBLING THE ROLLS

1. Combine the garlic, scallions, chiles, fish sauce, herbs, and lime juice in a small bowl. Peel the shrimp and, if you like, devein them. Spoon the seeds out of the cucumber halves and cut the halves crosswise so you have 4 sections. Cut each section lengthwise in half and then slice the halves, lengthwise, into strips between 1/8 and 1/4 inch thick—you need 75 strips. Put the strips in a bowl of ice water to help them keep their crunch.

2. Within a couple of hours of serving, set up a sheet pan with just enough water in it to coat the bottom. Place a sheet of rice paper in the sheet pan and let sit for about 30 seconds. **A:** Lift out the rice paper and place it on the work surface. **B:** Cover the half nearest you with part of a lettuce leaf. **C and D:** Place 3 strips of cucumber in the center pointing away from you and spoon a mounded tablespoon of the scallion–fish sauce– herb mixture over the lettuce and cucumber. **E and F:** Sprinkle with 2 teaspoons of peanuts and a small bunch of noodles—about 1/4 cup—along the cucumbers. **G:** Make three 1/4-inch-deep slits along the inside of the curve of the shrimp so the shrimp will be straight when you roll them. **H:** Place a shrimp, parallel with the cucumbers, on top. **I, J, and K:** Fold the bottom half of the rice

FOR THE DIPPING SAUCE

1/4 cup fish sauce, or more to taste

2 cloves garlic, minced and crushed to a paste with the side of a chef's knife

1/4 cup fresh lime juice (from about 2 limes)

1 tablespoon plus 1 teaspoon sugar, or more to taste

1 jalapeño or Thai "bird" chile, seeded and minced

FOR THE SUMMER ROLLS

6 ounces cellophane noodles (6 cups after soaking for 30 minutes)

2 cloves garlic, minced

16 scallions, white parts and 3 inches of the green parts, sliced fine

6 jalapeño chiles, seeded and chopped fine

3/4 cup fish sauce

leaves from 1 medium bunch basil, chopped just before using

leaves from one medium bunch mint, chopped just before using

1/4 cup fresh lime juice (from about 2 limes)

25 jumbo shrimp, boiled in the shell for 3 minutes, drained, and allowed to cool

1 long hothouse cucumber, peeled and cut in half lengthwise

twenty-five 8 1/2-inch rounds of rice paper

1/2 head iceberg lettuce

1/2 cup roasted peanuts, chopped coarse

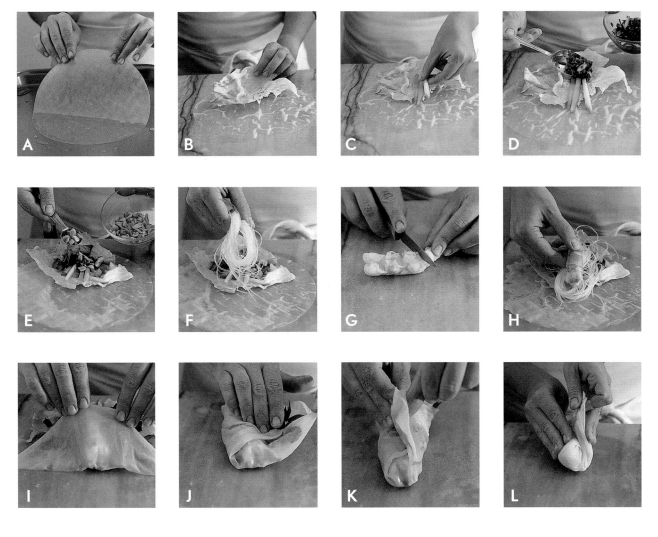

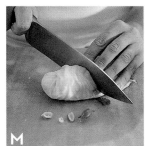

paper halfway up the cucumbers and fold over the sides to wrap the roll. **L:** Wrap the roll tightly. **M:** Cut the rolls in half on a bias. Place the finished rolls on a sheet pan lined with wax paper—to keep them from sticking—and keep them covered with a moist towel and refrigerated. Serve with the dipping sauce.

Shrimp Quesadillas

MAKES: 4 quesadillas (4 light main course servings)

Quesadillas are one of those formulaic things that you can alter according to what you have in the fridge. The only unalterable components are tortillas—usually flour, but corn are tastier—and cheese, authentically a mild Mexican style queso fresco, but more often Monterey Jack. Neither of these cheeses has a whole lot of flavor but that isn't the point; it's the mild melting effect that you're after. This version contains a salsa made with dried chiles, cilantro, and tomatoes. The salsa is also good served with grilled or smoked shrimp or other grilled foods.

1. Combine the chopped chiles with the tomatoes and cilantro. Season to taste with salt.

2. Brown the tortillas over medium to high heat in just enough oil to cover the bottom of a large sauté pan, about 2 minutes on each side. Spread 4 tortillas with the cheese, shrimp, and salsa and place a tortilla on top of each one so you have 4 quesadillas. (If you end up with extra salsa, serve it with the finished quesadillas.) Cook the quesadillas, 2 or more at a time (or all 4 at once if you have enough sauté pans) over low to medium heat; keep the first batch of quesadillas warm in the oven while you're making the others. Press down on the quesadillas with a spatula while they're in the sauté pan to help them glue together. Cook 5 to 7 minutes on each side until the cheese is completely melted. Cut into 4 wedges each. Serve with sour cream.

2 large dried chiles such as ancho, pasilla, guajillo, mulato, etc., soaked for 30 minutes in warm water and stemmed, seeded, and chopped fine

1 dried chipotle chile, soaked for 30 minutes in warm water, or 1 canned chipotle chile in adobo sauce, sauce rinsed off; stemmed, seeded, and chopped fine

4 medium tomatoes, stemmed, cut in half crosswise through the side, seeded, and chopped coarse

1 medium bunch cilantro, large stems removed, leaves and small stems chopped coarse

salt to taste

8 small corn tortillas

¼ cup olive oil

1 cup grated Monterey Jack cheese or other mild cheese

16 large shrimp, boiled for 2 minutes in the shell, peeled, deveined (deveining optional), each shrimp cut into 3 pieces

sour cream, crème fraîche, or queso fresco (for serving)

Shrimp "Samosas" with Sweet and Sour Chutney

MAKES: 24 samosas (24 hors d'oeuvre servings or 8 first course servings)

It's not really fair to call these samosas, the little fried packets encountered in India, because the dough for authentic samosas is made in an entirely different way from European pastry. These "samosas" are made with puff pastry, which gives a lovely flaky crust not shared by the real dish and a buttery flavor that lends a luxurious feeling to the final product. The authentic recipe is essentially a poor man's dish—most samosas are filled with a mixture composed predominantly of potatoes.

Making these samosas is somewhat of a project—even assuming you don't make your own puff pastry—but the advantage is that both they and the chutney can be made ahead and frozen. Ideally they should be frozen raw, thawed and kept in the refrigerator for up to a day before serving, and then deep-fried just before serving, but they're still fine even if fried before being frozen and then simply reheated in the oven.

Both the filling and the chutney for these samosas use the same spice mixture: garam masala. Indian cooks make a big batch at one time by first roasting the whole spices and then grinding them in a spice grinder or coffee grinder. If you make a lot of the mixture—it's a great substitute in recipes calling for off-the-shelf curry powder—it might be worth making a big batch and keeping it in the freezer. But for small amounts like those given here, it's easier to use ground spices (which have not been roasted) and to emulate the roasting technique by cooking them in a little oil or butter to get them to release their flavor.

PREPARING THE SPICE MIXTURE

Combine the spices for the spice mixture with the butter or oil in a small saucepan. Heat over low heat while stirring with a wooden spoon until fragrant, about 1 minute. Take off the heat.

FOR THE SPICE MIXTURE (GARAM MASALA)

1/4 teaspoon ground cardamom

1/4 teaspoon ground cinnamon

1/8 teaspoon ground cloves

1/2 teaspoon freshly ground pepper

1/2 teaspoon ground cumin

1/2 teaspoon ground coriander

2 tablespoons butter or vegetable oil

FOR THE FILLING

1 large Idaho potato, peeled

1 small red onion, chopped fine

2 tablespoons butter

one 2-inch piece fresh ginger, peeled and grated fine (half reserved for chutney)

1/2 cup frozen baby peas, thawed (optional)

6 jalapeño chiles, stemmed, seeded, and chopped fine (half reserved for chutney)

10 large shrimp, peeled, deveined, and cut into 1/3-inch dice

1 tablespoon fresh lemon juice

salt to taste

FOR THE CHUTNEY

6 ounces dried apricots, cut into
¼-inch dice

½ cup golden raisins (sultanas)

⅚ cup (½ plus ⅓) cup sugar

1 cup sherry vinegar

3 jalapeño chiles, stemmed, seeded,
and chopped fine (reserved from
filling recipe)

½ teaspoon salt or more to taste

FOR ASSEMBLING AND FRYING

2 pounds puff pastry

2 quarts vegetable oil

PREPARING THE FILLING

1. Cut the potato into 4 slices and put them in a pot with enough water to cover. Bring to a simmer and cook gently until the slices are easily pierced with a knife, about 20 minutes. Drain and let cool. Cut into ¼-inch dice.

2. Cook the onion in butter in a sauté pan over medium heat until translucent, about 12 minutes. Add half of the grated ginger, the peas, 2 teaspoons of the spice mixture, and half of the jalapeño chiles and cook for 1 minute more. Remove from the heat. Combine the onion mixture with the potatoes, shrimp, lemon juice, and salt. Refrigerate until well chilled.

PREPARING THE CHUTNEY

Combine the apricots, raisins, sugar, vinegar, salt, and the remaining chiles, spice mixture, and ginger in a small saucepan and simmer gently for 15 minutes or until lightly syrupy—like hot maple syrup. Let cool. Adjust the sweetness or sourness, if necessary, with sugar and vinegar. (If you add sugar you may need to heat the chutney to dissolve the sugar.) The chutney should be served cold; if it gets too stiff when it cools off, reheat it and add just enough water to thin it so it's a light syrup when hot.

ASSEMBLING THE SAMOSAS

Roll the puff pastry into 6 sheets, each measuring 6 x 12 inches and between ⅛- and 1/16-inch thick. Use a cookie cutter or jar lid to cut out two 6-inch rounds from each rectangle. Refrigerate the trimmings. **A:** Brush the rounds with cold water and cut them in half so you have a total of 24 semicircles; keep them cold. **B:** Fold one end of a half-circle over your thumb as you hold the dough. **C:** Wet the other half of the half-circle with water. **D and E:** Press the wet half of the half-circle over the other fold to form a cone. **F:** Hold the cone in your hand with the opening facing up. **G and H:** Place a mounded tablespoon of filling in the cone and press it in with a finger. **I:** Pinch the dough together along the large opening of the cone to form a triangle. Refrigerate or freeze until you're ready to fry. If you have extra filling, roll out the trimmings to make a few extra samosas.

FRYING AND SERVING

Heat the oil in a heavy pot—the oil shouldn't come more than halfway up the sides—to about 350°F. **J:** Gently lower in about 6 samosas—you can add more once you know how much the oil bubbles up—and use a spider utensil to gently turn them around in the oil so they brown evenly. If they're not surrounded by a lot of bubbles, the oil isn't hot enough; if they brown in less than a minute or brown unevenly, the oil is too hot. **K and L:** Fry the samosas for about 2 minutes, until golden brown, and drain on paper towels. Serve immediately with the chutney on the side.

Goat Cheese and Shrimp Chile Rellenos with Tomatillo Sauce

MAKES: 4 main course or 8 first course servings

8 fresh poblano chiles, charred, peeled (see page 20), stem left on

11 large shrimp, peeled, deveined (deveining optional), and cut into 3 pieces each

8 ounces goat cheese, crumbled or grated, or Monterey Jack, grated

FOR THE SAUCE

1 medium white or yellow onion, chopped

2 cloves garlic, minced

2 tablespoons olive oil or canola oil

1 dried chipotle chile, soaked for 30 minutes in warm water and drained, or 1 canned chipotle chile in adobo sauce, or 2 jalapeño chiles; stemmed, seeded, and chopped

2 fresh poblano chiles, charred, peeled (see page 20), stemmed, seeded, and chopped

2 pounds fresh tomatillos, sheaths removed, chopped coarse

½ bunch cilantro, large stems removed, leaves and small stems chopped fine

salt to taste

2 tablespoons fresh lime juice, or more to taste

The secret to great chile rellenos is to use poblano chiles, which have much more flavor than the usual bell peppers, and then, instead of deep-frying the chiles, gently sauté them in butter. The batter is lightened by beating the egg whites separately. The chiles are lightly floured before being coated with batter, which helps the batter stick. This recipe uses goat cheese but if you want something milder, use Monterey Jack or any other cheese you like.

PREPARING THE CHILES

Carefully make a small incision—about an inch-long slit—next to where the stem end enters the chiles without damaging or cutting through the rest of the chile. Leave the stems on. Rinse out the seeds—pull out the seeds that cling to the inside of the stem end—and pat dry. Put 4 pieces of shrimp and ⅛ of the cheese through the slit in each chile.

PREPARING THE SAUCE

In a small saucepan, cook the onion and garlic in the oil over medium heat. Stir every minute or so and adjust the heat so the onions turn shiny but don't brown—about 10 minutes. Add the chiles and the tomatillos and ¼ cup water. Cover the pot and simmer gently for 15 minutes. Add the cilantro and simmer 2 minutes more. Purée the sauce with an immersion blender or regular blender. Season with salt and lime juice to taste, keeping in mind that the cheese may be quite salty.

PREPARING THE BATTER AND COOKING THE CHILES

1. About 10 minutes before you're ready to serve, bring the sauce to a simmer and set up 2 sauté pans large enough to hold the chiles in a single layer without touching each other. Combine the egg whites with a pinch of salt and cream of tartar in a mixing bowl or bowl attachment to an electric mixer. Beat on slow speed for 1 minute and then on high speed for about 2 minutes—until the egg whites are fluffy but not yet stiff. In a small bowl, beat 4 of the egg yolks for about a minute by hand and fold them, using a rubber spatula, into the beaten whites. Dredge the stuffed chiles with flour—pat off any excess—and dip them in the batter. Make sure the chiles are well coated by using your hands to heap the batter over them.

2. Heat 2 tablespoons butter in each sauté pan over medium heat and gently arrange the chiles in the pans as you coat them with batter. Cook them over medium heat until golden brown on the first side, about 6 minutes, and gently turn them over. Cook them for about 6 minutes on the second side.

3. Place the sauce on heated plates—use enough to cover the plate—and put a chile or two on top. Serve immediately. Pass sour cream at the table.

FOR THE BATTER AND COOKING THE FILLED CHILES

6 eggs, separated

salt

tiny pinch cream of tartar unless you're using a copper bowl

½ cup flour

4 tablespoons butter

sour cream (for serving)

Shrimp with Smoked Salmon, Blinis, and Salmon Roe

MAKES: 4 first courses or 12 hors d'oeuvres (twelve 3-inch blinis)

These little pancakes—usually served with caviar—make a great hors d'oeuvre or, if you're serving just two or three people, a first course. Unlike most pancakes, blinis contain no chemical leavening such as baking powder but are lightened with yeast and beaten egg whites. Blinis can be made up to 2 days ahead and reheated just before serving.

1/3 cup milk

2 teaspoons sugar

1/2 teaspoon active dry yeast

1/2 cup all-purpose flour

1 egg, separated

1/2 teaspoon salt

6 tablespoons unsalted butter, or more as needed, or nonstick cooking spray

6 to 8 ounces very thinly sliced smoked salmon (about 8 slices large enough to make three 2- to 3-inch cutouts)

12 large shrimp, peeled and deveined

2 ounces salmon roe

6 tablespoons crème fraîche or sour cream

sprigs of dill, parsley, chervil, or fennel frond for garnish (optional)

PREPARING THE BLINIS

Warm the milk in a pan or in the microwave until it feels neither hot nor cold when you touch it with the back of your finger. Sprinkle the sugar and the yeast over the milk and stir. Let sit for 10 minutes. Add the flour and the egg yolk and mix with a whisk just long enough to make a smooth mixture. If you can't get out the lumps, strain the batter. Cover and let sit in a warm place for 1 hour or until the mixture is bubbly. Beat the egg white to soft peaks (when it's white and fluffy but drops off the whisk) and fold it into the batter along with the salt.

COOKING THE BLINIS

Heat a tablespoon of butter in a sauté pan, preferably nonstick, and spoon the batter into the pan in rounds, using about 2 tablespoons of batter. Cook the blinis over medium heat for about 3 minutes on the first side and 2 minutes on the second side. Keep the blinis warm in the oven while you make the second and third batches.

PREPARING THE SALMON AND ASSEMBLING THE BLINIS

1. Use a cookie cutter or glass to cut the smoked salmon into rounds the same size as the cooked blinis.

2. Sauté the shrimp in butter over medium heat for about 3 minutes.

3. Place a round of smoked salmon on each of the blinis, a shrimp in the center, and a mound of salmon roe on that. Top with a teaspoon of crème fraîche or pass the crème fraîche at the table. Decorate with one of the herbs, if desired.

baked dishes

Saganaki

MAKES: 6 first course or 4 main course servings

1 small onion, chopped fine

2 jalapeño chiles, stemmed, seeded, and minced

2 tablespoons olive oil

1 teaspoon dried oregano or 2 teaspoons fresh marjoram leaves

2 pounds ripe tomatoes, peeled, seeded (see page 21), and chopped coarse

30 large shrimp for first courses or 20 jumbo shrimp for main courses, peeled and deveined (deveining optional)

6 ounces feta or other crumbly goat cheese, crumbled

2 teaspoons ouzo (anisette-style liqueur), Pernod, or Ricard

1 small bunch parsley, large stems removed, leaves and small stems chopped fine just before serving

This is one of those dishes, now ubiquitous in Turkey, that, like tiramisu or crème brûlée in the United States, was nowhere to be found 50 years ago. This recipe calls for feta in keeping with "authentic" versions, but those who find that feta has an aggressive note can substitute a mild American or French goat cheese. The word saganaki *is the name of the vessel the dish is cooked and usually served in, a circular, metal shallow dish with handles. Copper versions can be found in cooking supply stores and while never cheap they're attractive enough to be useful for baking all sorts of foods—especially gratins—and then can be brought straight to the table.*

If you have a metal dish to serve the saganaki, use it to cook the onions and chiles in the oil over medium heat for about 10 minutes; otherwise use a saucepan. Add the oregano, cook for 1 more minute, and add the tomatoes. Turn the heat up to between medium and high and cook the sauce for about 10 minutes, stirring every minute or two, until it thickens. When you're ready to serve, fire up the broiler and nestle the shrimp in the hot sauce. Sprinkle the feta and ouzo over the shrimp and slide under the broiler. Broil for about a minute—keeping a close eye on it— until the cheese melts and bubbles. Sprinkle with parsley and serve.

Shrimp and Tarragon Custard

MAKES: 8 first course or side dish servings

This delicate custard makes an elegant first course or accompaniment to a main seafood course. You can garnish it with shrimp, mushrooms (wild mushrooms are dramatic), crayfish tails, fava beans, or anything you can think of. The trick with this custard—as with any custard—is to use the minimum amount of egg needed to get the custard to set without making it rubbery. The standard formula is one large egg to ¾ cup liquid (not including the egg), but here we push the limit for even more delicacy. Also be aware of the importance of slow, gentle cooking; if the custard gets too hot, the eggs set, release liquid, and the whole thing turns into a watery mess.

1. Preheat the oven to 275°F. Butter eight 4-ounce ramekins.

2. Bring the *Sauce Crevettes* to a simmer, add the heavy cream, and bring back to a simmer. Whisk together the eggs and strain into a medium bowl. Whisk the hot sauce mixture into the eggs off the heat until well combined. Rub the tarragon leaves with the olive oil and chop coarse. Add to the hot egg mixture, season to taste with salt and pepper, and let infuse for 15 minutes. Strain out the tarragon and ladle the hot mixture into the ramekins right away so the eggs don't settle.

3. Cover each ramekin with a small piece of aluminum foil to prevent a crust from forming in the oven. Put the ramekins in a baking pan with high sides and add enough boiling water to the pan so the water comes between one-third and halfway up the sides of the ramekins. Bake the custards until there's no longer any movement when you gently jiggle the custards from side to side—check more than one, as some may set more quickly than others because of variations in oven temperature—about 1 hour 15 minutes.

4. While the custards are baking, trim the mushrooms of any dark parts—if you're using wild mushrooms follow their contours so they retain their shape. If the mushrooms are large, cut cultivated mushrooms vertically in quarters; cut wild mushrooms depending on their size,

2 tablespoons softened butter
   (for the ramekins)

1 recipe (2 cups) *Sauce Crevettes*
   (page 173)

½ cup heavy cream

4 large eggs

leaves from 1 small bunch tarragon
   (about 40 leaves)

1 tablespoon olive oil

salt and pepper to taste

1 pound mushrooms, cultivated or wild,
   alone or in combination

½ pound fresh fava beans in the pod
   (or ½ cup fresh or frozen baby peas)

3 tablespoons butter

salt and pepper to taste

again following their shapes. Shuck the fava beans and blanch them for 1 minute in about 2 quarts of boiling water. Drain and rinse with cold water. Peel each bean individually. If you're using fresh peas, boil them for 1 minute and drain. If you're using frozen peas, just let them thaw—don't boil them as described on the box.

5. Take the ramekins out of the oven, let rest for 10 minutes, and unmold. If the custards don't pop out of the molds, run a knife around the side of the ramekins.

6. Sauté the mushrooms for about 10 minutes in the butter over medium to high heat, add the fava beans or peas, sauté for 2 minutes more, and season to taste with salt and pepper. Spoon this mixture over the custards as you serve.

Shrimp and Eggs "en Cocotte"

MAKES: 6 first course or light breakfast servings

One of the great and little appreciated dishes of French home cooking are eggs "en cocotte," or baked eggs. A whole egg is baked, usually with a little cream, in a small ramekin and then served with toast. Possibilities for variations are endless because different fillings can be placed into the ramekins before the egg and various sauces can be spooned over the eggs before baking. Shrimp is a natural choice and because the whole concoction is very moist, you can even get by using leftover shrimp. In the simplest version, just pour a little cream into the ramekins, put in the shrimp—diced or whole—grind over some pepper and salt, add a whole egg, and add some more cream and seasoning before baking. If you want to try more sophisticated variations, you can replace the cream (or some of it) with the Sauce Crevettes on page 173, with a creamy tomato sauce, or with a little saffron or curry infused in the cream. Also delicious is a little creamed spinach or even better, if you can find it, creamed sorrel, whose acidity cuts the richness of the whole dish. Chopped mushrooms, cooked down into what the French call duxelles, *give a rich and complex flavor.*

2 tablespoons butter, softened (for the ramekins)

1 tomato, peeled (see page 21), seeded, and chopped

1/4 teaspoon thyme leaves, chopped fine

1/2 cup heavy cream

16 large or 8 jumbo shrimp, peeled, deveined, cut into 1/2-inch dice

salt and pepper to taste

6 large eggs

buttered toast points (for serving)

1. Preheat the oven to 350°F.

2. Rub the insides of six 4- or 5-ounce ramekins with butter. Combine the tomato and thyme with the cream in a small saucepan and simmer it over medium heat for about 3 minutes or until the mixture just begins to thicken. Add the shrimp, stir, and remove from the heat. Season the shrimp mixture with salt and pepper to taste and spoon half of it into the ramekins.

3. Crack an egg into each of the ramekins and spoon over the remaining shrimp mixture. Put the ramekins in a baking pan with high sides and pour in enough boiling water to come 1/3 of the way up the sides of the ramekins. Bake until the egg white is no longer translucent and feels firm when you probe it with a fork, 12 to 15 minutes; the yolk should still be runny. Serve with buttered toast points.

Shrimp Gratin with Basil and Garlic

MAKES: 6 first course or 4 main course servings

18 jumbo shrimp for first courses or 16 jumbo shrimp for main courses, peeled and deveined (deveining optional)

½ cup (1 stick) unsalted butter

2 cloves garlic, minced and crushed to a paste with the side of a chef's knife

leaves from 1 small bunch basil

1 teaspoon salt

pepper to taste

2 tablespoons olive oil

1 slice firm-crumb white sandwich bread, crusts removed, processed to crumbs in a food processor

This isn't really a gratin—the shrimp are slowly baked, not broiled, so that a crust forms on top, and there's no cheese. Yet it is similar to a gratin in that the serving dishes must be heavy enough to keep the shrimp piping hot and the aroma of the pesto pungent and mouthwatering. The ideal serving dishes are heavy enameled iron and individually sized. You can also use a single serving dish—provided it's heavy—and just place it in the center of the table. A cheap and practical solution is to use a heavy iron skillet from any hardware store.

The trick to this recipe is to get the sauce and pan extremely hot without overcooking the shrimp or burning the butter. To avoid either, use frozen shrimp—don't thaw it ahead of time. In this way by the time the shrimp cooks through the pan will be burning hot and the butter frothy. You can cook and serve the shrimp in or out of their shells; they have more flavor in the shells but then your guests have to grapple with peeling the shrimp, something people in other countries don't seem to mind. But in all fairness, the shrimp are very hot and the sauce very drippy, so peeling the shrimp beforehand makes for easier eating.

1. If your shrimp aren't already frozen, spread the shrimp on a sheet pan and chill them well in the freezer for about 15 minutes—it's all right if they partially freeze. If you have frozen shrimp, let them thaw slightly at room temperature on the counter.

2. Cut the butter into 8 slices and put it in a food processor with the garlic, basil, salt, and some pepper. Purée for about 4 minutes. Initially you'll be stopping and starting and scraping down the sides of the food processor to get the mixture to move around, but persist until you can see that the basil is chopped fine within the butter. Wrap with plastic, roll into a cylinder, and chill.

3. Shortly before serving, preheat the oven to 450°F. Slice the butter cylinder into disks about the thickness of a quarter. Place the shrimp in one or more gratin dishes or other ovenproof dishes large enough to hold the shrimp in a single layer and bake the shrimp until they just start to turn red around the edges, about 3 minutes. Working quickly, cover the shrimp with the butter—spread the disks so they cover as much of the shrimp as possible—and sprinkle with the bread crumbs. Slide the dish(es) in the oven and bake until the shrimp is bright red and the butter is frothy, about 8 minutes. Serve immediately.

smoking, grilling, and barbecuing

Smoking

There are two kinds of smoking: hot smoking, in which the food is being cooked by the hot smoke, and cold smoking, in which the food is cured and smoked with cold smoke. Hot smoking is easier and can be done in any home kitchen in just a few minutes. Shrimp take well to smoking and, in fact, many of this book's recipes for soups and stews can be made with smoked shrimp to add a whole other flavor dimension.

There are several brands of home stove-top smokers on the market, but perhaps the easiest way to go about it is to improvise one with a circular wire cake rack, a wok or a sauté pan, and a lid. Put a couple of tablespoons of sawdust from fruit trees, hickory, or mesquite in the pan or wok, set the cake rack on top—if it's too large the outermost ring or two can be cut away with wire cutters—and the shrimp on top of that. Put the lid on and heat over high heat. The sawdust starts smoking almost immediately and completely smokes the shrimp in about 5 minutes.

Shrimp should be peeled before it's smoked so the smoke can reach the flesh. If you have head-on shrimp and want to present them that way, peel just the tails while leaving the heads on.

Smoked Shrimp

MAKES: 4 main course servings

In this recipe, the shrimp is cured to give it a crispier texture and a slight sweetness, which contrast well with the smokiness.

¼ cup salt

⅓ cup sugar

1 quart hot water

16 or 20 jumbo shrimp, peeled and deveined (deveining optional)

2 tablespoons sawdust such as hickory, fruit tree, mesquite, or food-grade wood chips

1. In a small bowl just large enough to hold the shrimp, dissolve the salt and sugar in the hot water and let cool to room temperature. Put the shrimp in the brine, ensuring that the brine completely covers the shrimp—and refrigerate for 4 hours or overnight.

2. Ten minutes before you're ready to serve, put the sawdust in the center of a wok or heavy-bottomed sauté pan—an iron skillet works well but you'll need to improvise a lid—and put the wok or pan on high heat.

Place a circular cake rack in the center of the pan or wok and arrange
the shrimp, in a single layer, on top. Cover the pan or wok and time for
5 minutes from the time you first smell smoke or see it drifting up
from under the lid. Serve immediately, either as is or accompanied by
the Aigrelette Sauce on page 48, the Roast Pepper and Chile Relish
on page 167, or any of the mayonnaises on pages 176–79.

SMOKING IN A LARGE COVERED BARBECUE

Many of us have Weber charcoal barbecues with covers that can double
as smokers. Because shrimp cook more quickly than most anything else
you're likely to grill or smoke, it's best to set the grill up so that the shrimp
is not directly over the coals. To do this, prepare a mound of coals and
push them to one side of the barbecue—even pile them up so there's a
large area on the bottom of the grill with no coals. **A and B:** Just before
smoking, place a sheet of aluminum foil on the coals and a handful of

sawdust on top or sprinkle the coals with a large handful of wet wood chips. Arrange the shrimp, on skewers as described on page 000, on the area of the grill below which there are no coals. Cover the grill and smoke for about 10 minutes, until the shrimp are bright red.

SMOKING IN A WOK

C and D: Place about 3 tablespoons of sawdust in the bottom of the wok, cover the sawdust with a small square of aluminum foil, and cover with a round cake rack. Put the wok on high heat. **E and F:** When the sawdust starts smoking, place the shrimp on the cake rack and cover the wok. Smoke for 3 to 5 minutes, depending on the size of the shrimp.

SMOKING IN A FRYING PAN

Select a heavy-bottomed skillet with a lid and a round cake rack with little feet that fits in the pan. Place 2 or 3 tablespoons of sawdust in the skillet and cover it loosely with a small square of aluminum foil. Put the pan on high heat until the sawdust starts to smoke, put in the cake rack, and arrange the shrimp on the cake rack. Cover the skillet and smoke for 3 to 5 minutes, depending on the size of the shrimp.

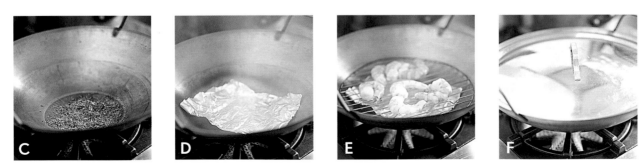

Grilling

Because shrimp cook so quickly they absorb very little scent of the grill. If you want them to have a smoky flavor it's better to use one of the techniques on pages 158–60.

The very best shrimp for grilling are wild Gulf shrimp grilled with their heads and shells on. Your guests can peel the shrimp themselves and suck the juices out of the heads. Because shrimp are relatively small, they should be threaded on two skewers so they can be easily and quickly turned over and taken off the grill (see photo, below). The skewers can be metal or wood, but if you use wooden skewers make sure the shrimp are pushed together so none of the wood is exposed; otherwise the wood will burn. If you don't want to light a fire, you can grill shrimp on the stove top in a cast-iron grill pan.

There are four ways to vary the flavor of grilled shrimp: by flavoring a brine for soaking the shrimp, by marinating the shrimp in something flavorful, by basting with something flavorful, and by serving with a tasty sauce.

Barbecuing

Barbecuing is really a combination of techniques and often includes grilling, smoking, braising, and steaming. Because shrimp cook very quickly, many of the techniques used for the slow barbecuing of meats won't work. In any case, buy the largest shrimp you can find so they will have as much time as possible on the grill, in the smoker, or in the oven before they overcook.

Tandoori Barbecued Shrimp

MAKES: 4 main course servings

The Indian technique called tandoori is usually used for the bright red chicken served in Indian restaurants, but it's easily adapted to shrimp. The long marinade in spice-scented yogurt and the flavorful paste used to coat the shrimp give it a marvelous flavor.

It seems that there are as many recipes for tandoori as there are cooks, but all the recipes have certain factors in common: They all call for long marinating, they all contain some source of heat, and most contain yogurt although some use heavy cream. Many recipes can be made with spices found at the supermarket while others call for black cardamom—which is more subtle than the usual green cardamom—Kashmiri chili powder (similar to paprika), and special spice mixtures meant to be sprinkled over the chicken just before serving. This version is made with easily found ingredients but gives options for more exotic ingredients for the more adventurous.

6 green cardamom pods or ½ teaspoon ground cardamom

2 tablespoons cumin seeds or ground cumin

1 tablespoon vegetable oil or ghee (see page 94; for cooking the spices)

½ teaspoon ground cloves

1 teaspoon freshly ground black pepper

3 jalapeño chiles or 2 Thai "bird" chiles, stemmed, seeded, and minced

1 clove garlic, minced

one 1-inch piece fresh ginger, peeled and grated fine

½ cup plain yogurt

2 tablespoons paprika

salt to taste

16 jumbo shrimp (the largest you can find), peeled and deveined

3 tablespoons melted butter or ghee (see page 94; for basting)

3 lemon wedges

1. If you're using cardamom in the pods and whole cumin, take the little seeds out of the cardamom pods, combine them with the whole cumin in a coffee grinder, and grind for 1 minute. Heat the vegetable oil or ghee in a small saucepan and stir in the freshly ground spices. Cook over low to medium heat for about 1 minute until fragrant. Take off the heat and add the cloves, pepper, chiles, garlic, ginger, yogurt, paprika, and salt to taste. Refrigerate while you're preparing the shrimp.

2. Cut 3 diagonal slashes about ¼ inch deep into the side of each shrimp on both sides. Put the shrimp in the marinade and stir until it's thoroughly coated. Refrigerate for 12 to 24 hours before grilling.

3. When you're ready to grill or broil, wipe the marinade off the shrimp and put 4 shrimp on each of 4 pairs of skewers. If you're using wooden skewers, be sure to push the shrimp together so they touch or the wood in between the shrimp will burn. Brush the shrimp with the butter or ghee and then with the remaining marinade and grill or broil over high heat for about 2 minutes on each side. Sprinkle with lemon juice.

A NOTE ABOUT SPICES: Indian cooks almost always roast their spices the day they use them. Since this can be a nuisance, especially when you only need a little, it's worthwhile to roast a bottle of a particular spice (always buy the smallest amount you can) by stirring it in a sauté pan on the stove until it smells toasty and fragrant and then storing it in the freezer. Most spices can be ground in a coffee grinder, but again you'll need to grind enough for the blades to reach. If you're buying ground spices—which have not been roasted—cook what you need in a little ghee or vegetable oil until they are fragrant.

New Mexico Barbecue

MAKES: 6 main course servings

The flavor of barbecued foods comes from the smoke of the grill and the flavors of the marinade and sauce. Often, the marinade and sauce are the same thing, as in this version of a New Mexico–style barbecue sauce. Since shrimp cook very quickly, unlike ribs or other slow-cooking barbecued foods, it's best to set up the grill with a low fire pushed to one side and just before grilling or smoking place wet twigs on the fire. In this way the shrimp can absorb smoke for 15 minutes without overcooking.

3 tablespoons olive oil

1 small red onion, chopped

2 cloves garlic, minced

6 medium tomatoes, peeled, seeded, and chopped

1 dried chipotle chile, soaked for 30 minutes in warm water, or 1 canned chipotle chile in adobo sauce, sauce rinsed off, or 2 jalapeño chiles; stemmed, seeded, and chopped coarse

2 dried pasilla chiles, stemmed, soaked for 30 minutes in warm water, seeded, and chopped coarse

1 dried ancho chile, stemmed, soaked for 30 minutes in warm water, seeded, and chopped coarse

¼ cup ketchup

2 tablespoons Dijon mustard

3 tablespoons honey

1 tablespoon Worcestershire sauce

salt to taste

30 large or 24 jumbo shrimp, peeled and deveined (deveining optional)

3 tablespoons melted butter

1. Heat the oil over medium heat in a saucepan and add the onion and garlic. Cook for about 10 minutes, or until the onion turns translucent.

2. Add the tomatoes to the onion mixture and cook over medium heat until the mixture thickens, about 15 minutes. Stir in the rest of the ingredients and let cool. Marinate the shrimp for 4 to 24 hours in ¼ of the sauce.

3. When you're ready to grill, wipe the marinade off the shrimp and put 4 or 5 shrimp each on 6 pairs of skewers (see photo on page 161). Brush with melted butter and grill, away from direct heat, for about 15 minutes. Brush every couple of minutes with butter and the remaining sauce. Heat the sauce and place 2 or 3 tablespoons in the center of 6 heated plates. Arrange the shrimp on top. Pass the extra sauce.

SMOKING: Instead of grilling or broiling, you can lightly smoke these shrimp by cooking them in a covered barbecue with wood chips.

Lightly Smoked Shrimp with Honey Mustard Marinade

MAKES: 12 hors d'oeuvre servings, 4 first course servings, or 4 main course servings

You can make this shrimp dish in an improvised stove-top smoker or in a covered barbecue with the coals moved to one side (see pages 158–60). The shrimp are best when marinated overnight but in a pinch you can get by with an hour or two. If you're serving these as an hors d'oeuvre, buy medium shrimp and skewer them with toothpicks or put them on baguette toasts like the bruschetta on page 53.

1. Make 3 diagonal slashes on each side of the shrimp, about ¼ inch deep for jumbo shrimp or ⅛ inch deep for large shrimp.

2. In a mixing bowl large enough to hold the shrimp, stir together the remaining ingredients except for the olive oil and pour them over the shrimp. Stir the mixture until the shrimp is well coated and let marinate in the refrigerator for 2 to 24 hours.

3. When you're ready to grill, wipe the marinade off the shrimp and mix them together with the olive oil. Smoke in a covered barbecue with the coals piled to one side and wet wood chips sprinkled over them or in a stove-top smoker. Serve with the Roast Pepper and Chile Relish on page 167, the Tropical Fruit Salsa on page 172, or the mayonnaises on pages 176–79.

20 large shrimp for hors d'oeuvres or first courses or 20 jumbo shrimp for main courses, peeled and deveined

3 tablespoons honey

1 tablespoon Tabasco or other hot sauce

2 tablespoons Dijon mustard or whole grain mustard (preferably Maille brand)

1 dried chipotle chile, soaked for 30 minutes in warm water and drained, or 1 canned chipotle chile in adobo sauce, or 2 jalapeño chiles; stemmed, seeded, and chopped coarse

¼ cup balsamic vinegar

2 teaspoons fresh marjoram leaves or ½ teaspoon fresh thyme leaves

1 teaspoon salt

2 tablespoons olive oil

handful of sawdust such as hickory, fruit tree, mesquite, or food-grade wood chips

Barbecued Shrimp with Smoked Tomato Sauce

MAKES: 6 main course servings

This dish mimics the flavor of barbecued ribs by smoking the ingredients for the sauce ahead of time and then using the sauce to cook the shrimp. You can make the sauce the same day you serve the shrimp, but it's a good idea to smoke the tomatoes after a barbecue while the fire still has plenty of life in it. The sauce will keep several days in the refrigerator. Cornbread is a great accompaniment.

12 ripe tomatoes, cut in half crosswise and seeded

2 tablespoons olive oil

2 poblano chiles, charred and peeled

1 dried chipotle chile, soaked for 30 minutes in warm water and drained, or 1 canned chipotle chile in adobo sauce, sauce rinsed off, or 2 jalapeño chiles, stemmed, seeded, and finely chopped

¼ cup balsamic vinegar

2 teaspoons sugar or more to taste

salt (omit if shrimp has been brined) and pepper to taste

24 jumbo shrimp, peeled and deveined

4 cups hickory (or other hardwood) sawdust, plus more as needed

1. Prepare coals in a covered barbecue and push them into a pile to one side.

2. Put the olive oil on a plate and dip the flat side of the tomato halves in it to keep the tomatoes from sticking to the grill grate. Place about 2 cups of hickory or other hardwood sawdust on a sheet of aluminum foil over the coals. Arrange the tomatoes, flat side down, on the grill away from the coals, and cover the grill. Smoke in this way until you no longer see smoke coming out of the holes on top of the grill, usually about 10 minutes. Pour in another 2 cups of sawdust and continue in this way, adding sawdust as needed, until the tomatoes have softened but haven't turned into mush, about 30 minutes. Use a large spoon to gently remove the tomatoes from the grill.

3. Work the tomatoes through a food mill or strainer into a large saucepan, combine with the chiles, and simmer over medium heat, stirring to prevent sticking, until the sauce thickens, about 20 minutes. Add half the vinegar and sugar, stir, and taste. Add the rest only if you feel the sauce needs it. Season to taste with salt and pepper.

4. Grill, smoke, or sauté the shrimp and add it to the hot sauce. Serve on heated plates.

Roast Pepper and Chile Relish

MAKES: about 2 cups (enough for 8 main course servings)

This relish is a great accompaniment to grilled or smoked shrimp. You can improvise your own variations on this relish by using different chiles and herbs, but be wary of making it too hot by including at least a couple of bell peppers, preferably red or yellow, to add color. Don't add the vinegar or sugar all at once as you may like it more or less sweet or tangy. Because of the vinegar, this relish can be made ahead and will keep in the refrigerator for a month or more.

Toast the dried chiles in a heavy skillet over medium heat for about 2 minutes on each side—until they are fragrant and become pliable—then stem them and cut them in half lengthwise. Soak them in warm water for 30 minutes and chop fine. Combine all the ingredients and serve or refrigerate for a month or more.

3 bell peppers, preferably red, yellow, or orange, charred, peeled (see page 20), stemmed, seeded, and cut into ¼-inch dice

2 poblano chiles, charred, peeled, stemmed, seeded, and cut into ¼-inch dice

1 or 2 dried chipotle chiles, soaked for 30 minutes in warm water and drained, or 1 or 2 canned chipotle chiles in adobo sauce, sauce rinsed off, or 2 to 4 jalapeño chiles; stemmed, seeded, and chopped fine

4 dried chiles, such as ancho, guajillo, mulato, pasilla de Oaxaca, or chihuacles negros, preferably a combination

¼ cup vinegar

4 teaspoons sugar

1 teaspoon dried oregano, preferably Mexican oregano, chopped fine just before using

salt to taste

Salsas vs. Relishes

The distinctions between sauces, salsas, chutneys, and relishes are often confusing and don't really matter much, but it's safe to generalize by saying that salsas are usually made with raw ingredients and remain uncooked; chutneys often contain cooked ingredients combined with a sweetener and an acidic element; and relishes are usually made with pickled ingredients and contain a fair amount of salt.

1 medium red onion, chopped fine

3 cloves garlic, minced and crushed to a
    paste with the side of a chef's knife

3 tablespoons peanut oil, vegetable oil,
    or butter

2 Thai "bird" chiles or jalapeño chiles,
    stemmed, seeded, and minced

2 teaspoons ground coriander

1 teaspoon ground cumin

1 teaspoon ground turmeric

1/8 teaspoon ground nutmeg

1 teaspoon ground cinnamon

1 teaspoon ground cardamom

2 tablespoons soy sauce

one 1/2-inch piece fresh ginger, peeled
    and grated fine

1/3 cup smooth natural peanut butter
    (should contain only peanuts and salt)

1 teaspoon shrimp paste (*terasi*) or more
    to taste (optional)

6 kaffir lime leaves, chopped fine (optional)

2 teaspoons sugar

one 14-ounce can unsweetened
    coconut milk

2 tablespoons fresh lime juice,
    or more to taste

salt to taste

30 large or 24 jumbo shrimp for first
    courses, 24 large or 20 jumbo shrimp
    for main courses, peeled and deveined
    (deveining optional)

Shrimp Saté

MAKES: 6 first course or 4 main course servings

A saté is a combination of a sauce, a marinade, and grilled food on skewers. Most saté sauces contain peanuts, coconut milk, and chiles but after that recipes vary wildly. While satés are Indonesian, many of the flavorings are also found in Thai cooking. Much of the heart and soul of Indonesian cooking in general—not just their seafood cooking—relies on a shrimp paste the Indonesians call terasi. *This paste is so pungent that it makes fish sauce smell like roses. You can certainly leave it out—the dishes are perfectly fine without it—but if you want to give your food a maximum of authenticity, use the* terasi. *One way around the lingering odors is to put the paste in a little packet of aluminum foil and heat the packet in a sauté pan for a couple of minutes. Once it's cooled, stir it into your sauce, soup, or stew. You can also dispense with the precooking—it you want more shrimp paste flavor, just use more.*

1. Cook the onion and garlic in the oil over medium heat until translucent, about 10 minutes. Add the chiles and the spices and cook until you can smell the spices, about 1 minute more. Stir in the soy sauce, ginger, peanut butter, shrimp paste, lime leaves, sugar, coconut milk, lime juice, and salt to taste. Stir until smooth, bring to a simmer, and let cool. Use about 1/3 of this sauce to marinate the shrimp. Cover and refrigerate the shrimp in its marinade for 2 hours or overnight.

2. When you're ready to grill, wipe the marinade off the shrimp and thread them on pairs of skewers. If you're using wooden skewers, be sure the shrimp are touching so the wood doesn't burn in between them. Grill for 2 to 3 minutes on each side and serve with the remaining marinade, heated.

Shrimp with Leeks and Mushrooms

MAKES: 6 first course servings

You can make this simple dish with regular cultivated mushrooms—but cremini, the slightly browner ones, have more flavor and are usually about the same price. To turn this dish into something extremely elegant, use as many kinds of wild mushrooms as you can find.

1. Cut green ends of the leeks off, leaving 1 inch of pale green; cut off the hairy root end and discard. Slice the leeks in half lengthwise and hold each half under running water, folding back the leaves to rinse out any sand. Cut about 1/2 inch away from the base of the leeks so the individual membranes peel away from the center, and julienne the leeks. Heat 2 tablespoons of butter in a medium sauté pan over medium-low heat and cook the leeks, covered, stirring frequently, for about 20 minutes, until completely soft but not brown.

2. While the leeks are cooking, rinse off the mushrooms in a colander. Depending on their size, leave them whole or cut them in halves or quarters. If you're using cultivated mushrooms that are larger than button mushrooms, cut them vertically into quarters—don't slice them. If you're using wild mushrooms, follow their natural contours so that once they're cut you still have a sense of their shape.

3. Sauté the mushrooms in the remaining 2 tablespoons butter over medium to high heat for about 5 minutes. Remove from the heat, sprinkle with the parsley and salt and pepper to taste, and reserve.

4. When the leeks are soft, pour in the cream and turn the heat to high. Stir while the cream simmers, just long enough to coat the leeks, about 2 minutes. Season to taste with salt and pepper. Sauté, grill, or smoke the shrimp. Place a mound of mushrooms in the center of 6 heated plates and a mound of leeks on top. Place a shrimp on top of the leeks. Decorate each plate with a sprig of chervil, parsley, dill, or fennel frond, if desired.

3 medium leeks

4 tablespoons butter

3/4 pound mushrooms, preferably an assortment

1/2 small bunch parsley, large stems removed, leaves and small stems chopped very fine

salt and pepper to taste

1/2 cup heavy cream

6 jumbo shrimp, peeled and sautéed, grilled, or smoked

6 sprigs chervil, parsley, dill, or fennel frond (optional)

sauces

Poblano Chile Sauce Shrimp

MAKES: 2 cups (enough for 8 servings of shrimp)

Combining this sauce with grilled, smoked, or sautéed shrimp makes a delightfully bright and colorful first course. The sauce is very simple: Peeled poblano chiles are chopped and infused with a little cream and bacon. The bacon provides a smoky note that complements the grilled flavor of the shrimp. This recipe makes 2 cups, enough for about 1/4 cup each for 8 people—more than a normal amount of sauce, but this sauce is so good that your guests will end up practically licking their plates.

Cut the bacon strips crosswise into 1/4-inch-wide strips. Cook them over low to medium heat in a small saucepan until they turn crispy, about 10 minutes, or put them on a plate, cover with a paper towel and microwave until crispy, about 2 minutes. If you cooked the bacon in a pan, pour out and discard the fat by holding the bacon back with a slotted spoon. If you used the microwave, put the bacon bits in a small saucepan. Add the poblano chiles and the cream and simmer over medium heat for about 7 minutes until the sauce is the thickness you like. Add the rest of the peppers to the cream mixture and simmer again for a couple of minutes to thicken. Add the vinegar, simmer 1 minute more, and season to taste with salt. Stir in the cilantro. If you want to be formal, spoon 2 or 3 tablespoons of sauce in the center of 8 heated plates and arrange cooked shrimp on top. Spoon a little sauce over the shrimp. Otherwise, just pass the sauce at the table.

2 strips bacon

2 poblano chiles, charred, peeled (see page 20), stemmed, seeded, chopped fine, and crushed to a paste with the side of a chefs' knife

1 1/3 cups heavy cream

1 red bell pepper, charred, peeled (see page 20), stemmed, seeded, and cut into fine dice

1 yellow or orange bell pepper, charred, peeled (see page 20), stemmed, seeded, and cut into fine dice

1 green Cuban pepper or regular green bell pepper, charred, peeled (see page 20), stemmed, seeded, and chopped fine

4 teaspoons sherry vinegar or wine vinegar, or more to taste

salt to taste

1 tablespoon cilantro, chopped fine

Tropical Fruit Salsa

MAKES: 5 cups (enough for 12 servings of grilled or cold shrimp), with leftover pineapple

1 mango (about 1 pound)

1 pineapple, preferably "golden"

1 Hawaiian or ½ Mexican papaya

1 medium red onion, sliced thin

1 tablespoon salt, plus more to taste

2 dried chipotle chiles, soaked for 30 minutes in warm water and drained, or 2 canned chipotle chiles in adobo sauce, sauce rinsed off, or 2 jalapeño chiles; stemmed, seeded, and chopped fine

2 poblano chiles, charred, peeled (see page 20), stemmed, seeded, and chopped fine

1 medium bunch cilantro, large stems removed, chopped just before serving

3 tablespoons fresh lime juice

1 small bunch basil, preferably "holy" basil, chopped just before serving (optional)

1 small bunch mint, chopped just before serving (optional)

This salsa is hot, sweet, and sour and makes a perfect sauce for cold shrimp—a great twist on traditional shrimp cocktail—or for shrimp sizzling hot off the grill. In a more elegant hors d'oeuvre preparation, you can serve it in combination with the Sauce Crevettes, opposite. This recipe makes 5 cups of salsa, so unless you're having lots of guests, you may want to make a half batch and save the rest of the fruit for some tropical daiquiris.

1. Peel the mango and cut the flesh away from the pit, then cut the flesh into ½-inch dice. Twist the stem off the pineapple and stand it on end. Cut down around the sides, deep enough to cut under the little pits, until you've removed all the peel. Cut it lengthwise in quarters and cut away the strip of core that runs along each of the wedges. Cut the quarters into strips about ¼-inch wide on each side; slice the strips into dice. Peel the papaya, cut it in half lengthwise, and spoon out the seeds. Cut it lengthwise into thin wedges and cut the wedges into strips; slice the strips into dice.

2. Sprinkle the onion slices with the salt and rub them between your hands until you no longer feel the salt. Drain in a colander for 15 minutes. Wring out as much liquid as you can by squeezing small bunches of the slices in your fists.

3. Toss together all the ingredients and season to taste with salt.

Creamy Shrimp Sauce
(Sauce Crevettes)

MAKES: about 2 cups

Rinse off the shrimp heads and shake dry. Heat the oil, over high heat, in a wide-bottomed pot large enough to hold the heads in a single layer. When the oil just begins to smoke, add the heads—stand back, they can splatter. Stir with a wooden spoon until the heads turn red, about 5 minutes. Transfer the heads to a food processor. Turn the heat down to medium and stir in the onion and tomatoes. Cover the pan and cook, covered, for 10 minutes. Purée the heads for 30 to 45 seconds. Pour the cognac, if using, into the pan with the tomatoes—stand back while it boils down so it doesn't flare up in your face—and add the wine. Stir in the head mixture, and add the herbs and the cream. Cook at a low simmer for 30 minutes, stirring every few minutes. Work the mixture through a regular strainer and then again through a fine-mesh strainer. If you're using Pernod, add it now. Season to taste with salt and pepper.

2 quarts shrimp heads (about 1 pound)

3 tablespoons olive oil

1 medium onion, chopped fine

4 tomatoes, chopped coarse

¼ cup cognac (optional)

½ cup white wine

5 sprigs fresh tarragon

3 sprigs fresh thyme

2 cups heavy cream

1 teaspoon Pernod (optional)

salt and pepper to taste

Types of Sauces

There are two types of sauces: those that contrast with the central element (for example, shrimp) and really function like condiments, and those that underline and bring into focus the flavor of the central element. Most Asian sauces are of the first type. They're usually full-flavored and often spicy. When well conceived, such a sauce can accent an ingredient by juxtaposing hot with cool, spicy with mild, or sour with sweet. The second kind of sauce is one that extracts and amplifies the flavor of the main ingredient—like shrimp heads. For any shrimp sauce to taste like shrimp—ideally it would taste more like shrimp than the shrimp itself—you'll need the shrimp heads or a good collection of shells.

Mango Chutney with Raisins and Almonds

MAKES: about 1 ½ cups, enough for 25 shrimp

This recipe is adapted from Julie Sahni's Classic Indian Vegetarian and Grain Cooking, *a book crammed with tasty ideas for even the nonvegetarian. In her introduction to the recipe, Ms. Sahni explains that this special and expensive chutney is reserved for grand occasions in India. A recommendation: Buy an ounce of saffron at a time. It will cost about five times as much as one of those little vials but will last for years. I like to serve this chutney with grilled shrimp.*

Peel the mango and cut the flesh away from the pit. Purée the pulp with the salt in a food processor and transfer to a heavy-bottomed saucepan. Add the saffron with its soaking liquid and add the rest of the ingredients. Bring to a gentle simmer and cook, stirring every couple of minutes, until the mixture is thick and syrupy, about 20 minutes. Store in the refrigerator and serve cold or at room temperature.

1 large underripe mango (about 1 pound)

1 ½ teaspoons coarse salt

½ teaspoon saffron threads, soaked for 30 minutes in 1 tablespoon water

4 jalapeño chiles or 2 Thai "bird" chiles, stemmed, seeded, and minced

½ teaspoon ground cardamom

⅛ teaspoon ground cloves

2 teaspoons ground cumin

3 tablespoons golden raisins (sultanas)

3 tablespoons slivered almonds, toasted for about 12 minutes in a 350°F oven

2 tablespoons fresh lime juice

2 tablespoons brown sugar

Mint or Cilantro Raita

MAKES: 1 2/3 cups

Variations of raita—the Indian name for cucumber in yogurt—can be found throughout the Middle East and of course in India. Raita is often served with a hot Indian meal to cut the heat and richness, but it can also be used as a refreshing salsa to counterbalance grilled or smoked shrimp.

1. Line a large strainer with a triple layer of cheesecloth and spoon in the yogurt. Set the strainer over a bowl and refrigerate for 2 hours or overnight.

2. Slice the cucumber lengthwise into 8 strips. Slice the strips so you end up with cubes that are about 1/4 inch on each side. In a mixing bowl, sprinkle the salt over the cucumber cubes and rub the cubes between your hands until you no longer feel the salt. Drain in a colander for 30 minutes to an hour.

3. Squeeze the cucumber cubes in your fists as hard as you can to extract as much liquid as possible.

4. Chop the cilantro or mint and add it to the cucumbers. Stir in the yogurt, lime juice, and chopped chiles and season to taste with salt and pepper.

2 cups plain yogurt, preferably whole milk

1 hothouse cucumber, peeled, halved lengthwise, seeds scooped out with a spoon

1 tablespoon coarse salt

1 dried chipotle chile, soaked for 30 minutes in warm water and drained, or 1 canned chipotle chile in adobo sauce, sauce rinsed off, or 2 jalapeño chiles; stemmed, seeded, and chopped fine

1 medium bunch cilantro or mint, large stems removed

3 tablespoons fresh lime juice

salt and pepper to taste

Assorted Mayonnaises

Most of us associate mayonnaise with the stuff in a jar or, if we're fortunate, an aioli sauce with plenty of garlic. It turns out, however, that mayonnaise is an infinitely versatile sauce that can be flavored with just about anything. The base for all these variations, however, is almost always the same, so once you make a batch of basic unflavored mayonnaise, you can divide it into however many parts you like and flavor the parts.

Basic mayonnaise can be made by hand—by slowly working oil into egg yolks—in a blender, or in a food processor. There are a couple of things to look out for. Mayonnaise gets thicker as you add more oil, but if it gets too thick it can separate. So whatever recipe you're making, add 1/2 teaspoon of water to the mayonnaise if it starts to get too thick. Don't add too much water—it takes very little to thin the mayonnaise and keep it from breaking. When you start making the mayonnaise, the oil has to added slowly—in a very thin stream for a food processor or blender and 1 teaspoon at a time when working by hand. Mayonnaise such as aioli, made with extra virgin olive oil, should not be beaten hard by hand, in a blender, or in a food processor—for some reason the violent action makes it bitter. It's better to make a basic mayonnaise with vegetable oil and then gently stir in extra virgin olive oil by hand. (For more about this method, see page 179.) While mayonnaise is rich—the mayonnaise itself is almost pure oil—it is considerably lighter when combined with vegetables, which convert it into something between a mayonnaise and a salsa.

Basic Mayonnaise

MAKES: 2 1/2 cups

2 egg yolks

2 teaspoons fresh lemon juice

2 teaspoons Dijon mustard

1/2 teaspoon salt, plus more to taste

1 cup "pure" olive oil or vegetable oil

1/2 cup extra virgin olive oil

2 to 4 tablespoons water

Combine the egg yolks, lemon juice, mustard, and salt in a food processor or blender. Turn the machine on and start by adding the oil very slowly, in a thin stream, and then gradually increasing the amount you add. When you've added all the "pure" oil and the mayonnaise starts to thicken, transfer the mayonnaise to a bowl and gently work in the extra virgin olive oil using a wooden spoon. As the mayonnaise gets very thick, add water as needed. Add more salt if needed.

Red Bell Pepper Mayonnaise

MAKES: 1 ¾ cups

Combine the peppers with the Basic Mayonnaise and season to taste with salt and pepper.

4 red bell peppers, charred, peeled (see page 20), stemmed, seeded, and chopped fine

1 cup Basic Mayonnaise

salt and pepper to taste

Mushroom Mayonnaise

MAKES: 2 cups

Clean the mushrooms and chop by hand or in a food processor until fairly fine. Be careful if you're using a food processor to avoid making a purée; about 10 short pulses should do it. Put the mushrooms in a small pot over medium heat. When they've released their water, after 1 to 2 minutes, turn the heat up to high and boil, stirring now and then, until the mixture is dry, about 10 minutes. Let cool and fold into the Basic Mayonnaise. Season to taste with salt and pepper.

1 pound mushrooms of any variety

1 cup Basic Mayonnaise

salt and pepper to taste

Morel Mayonnaise

MAKES: 1 ½ cups

Regular mushroom mayonnaise is great but dried morels give this mayonnaise a distinctive smoky flavor.

Drain the morels into a bowl, squeezing any additional liquid out of them; note that you can save the liquid for sauces, but don't add it to the mayonnaise unless you want it to be thin. Chop the morels fine by hand or in a food processor—avoid overprocessing and turning them into a paste—and stir them into the Basic Mayonnaise. Season to taste with salt and pepper.

1 ounce dried morels, soaked in ½ cup water for 30 minutes and moved around every 5 minutes

1 cup Basic Mayonnaise

salt and pepper to taste

Caper and Herb Mayonnaise

MAKES: 1 3/4 cups

1 cup Basic Mayonnaise (see page 176)

1 tablespoon Dijon mustard

4 tablespoons capers, drained and chopped coarse

leaves from 15 sprigs fresh tarragon, chopped

1 small bunch parsley, large stems removed, leaves and small stems chopped

salt and pepper to taste

Combine the Basic Mayonnaise with the other ingredients. Season with salt and pepper to taste.

Hazelnut Mayonnaise

MAKES: 1 1/4 cups

1/4 cup hazelnut oil made from roasted nuts (Le Blanc is a good brand)

1 cup Basic Mayonnaise (see page 176)

salt and pepper to taste

This mayonnaise catches people by surprise because it's redolent of hazelnuts but there are no hazelnuts in it. Only a small amount of hazelnut oil is worked into a basic mayonnaise. It's important to use a hazelnut oil that's been made with roasted nuts—it will have much more flavor and be far less perishable. As of now there is only one producer—Le Blanc—who makes his oil this way. It's expensive, too, so unless you use a lot of it, buy the smallest amount possible and keep it in the freezer.

Mix the oil, a few teaspoons at a time, into the Basic Mayonnaise. Season to taste with salt and pepper. If you like, you can color the mayonnaise green with chlorophyll (see page 182).

Curry Mayonnaise

MAKES: 1 cup

Heat the oil and curry powder in a small pan over medium heat while stirring until you smell the curry, about 1 minute. Stir this mixture into the Basic Mayonnaise. Taste to judge if the amount of curry is enough; if not, heat some more and add it to the mayonnaise. If the mayonnaise starts to get too thick (which can cause it to break) thin it with a teaspoon or two of water. Stir in the cilantro.

1 tablespoon vegetable oil
(or more as needed)

1 tablespoon curry powder
(or more as needed)

2 tablespoons cilantro, chopped fine
(optional)

1 cup Basic Mayonnaise (see page 176)

Saffron Aioli

MAKES: 2½ cups

In a large mixing bowl, whisk together the egg yolks, lemon juice, and teaspoon of salt. Add the saffron with its soaking liquid and beat in the garlic and "pure" olive oil with a whisk. (Alternatively, you can use a food processor.) Start by adding the oil very slowly and then gradually increase the amount you add at one time. When you've added all the "pure" oil, and the mayonnaise starts to thicken, transfer the mayonnaise to a mixing bowl (if you were using a food processor) and gently work in the extra virgin olive oil using a wooden spoon. Add more salt if needed. (See also "Fixing" Bottled Mayonnaise, page 176.)

TIPS FOR MAKING AIOLI: Aioli is garlic mayonnaise traditionally made with a mortar and pestle, but most versions now are made in a blender, food processor, or by hand with a whisk. The problem with any method but the mortar and pestle is that the hard beating action turns the extra virgin olive oil bitter. One solution is to work the oil very gently into the egg yolks with a wooden spoon, but this is tedious since the oil has to be added very slowly. Another solution is to make a mayonnaise with "pure" olive oil—which is essentially flavorless and doesn't turn bitter when beaten—using a hand whisk. Once the mayonnaise has established itself, and you can add the oil more quickly, switch to a wooden spoon to gently work in the extra virgin olive oil.

4 egg yolks

4 teaspoons fresh lemon juice

1 teaspoon salt, plus more as needed

1 teaspoon saffron threads soaked in
3 tablespoons water for 30 minutes

3 medium cloves garlic, chopped and
crushed with the side of a chef's knife

1 cup "pure" olive oil or vegetable oil

1 cup extra virgin olive oil

Coconut Chutney

MAKES: 2 cups sauce (enough for about 12 servings—extra sauce freezes well)

2 cups fresh coconut pieces or 2 cups dried, grated unsweetened coconut

1 large bunch cilantro, large stems removed

one 1-inch piece fresh ginger, peeled and grated fine

2 cloves garlic, minced and crushed to a paste with the side of a chef's knife

3 jalapeño chiles, stemmed, seeded, and minced

3 tablespoons fresh lemon juice

2 teaspoons ground coriander

½ teaspoon ground cloves

½ teaspoon ground cinnamon

2 teaspoons sugar

one 14-ounce can unsweetened coconut milk

1 medium red onion, chopped fine

salt to taste

One of the secrets to making a single ingredient like shrimp exciting and varied is to serve it with a variety of sauces and condiments. To dramatize this effect, use an assortment of different bowls or buy a thali. *A* thali *is a tray with little metal cups that line its perimeter and is also the name of a kind of Indian dinner where five, seven, or even more dishes are served at the same time. In principle one is supposed to work around the circle, sampling flavors, and end with a sweet, but it's more fun to go back and forth and experience different juxtapositions. This dish can be made with fresh or dried coconut; getting the flesh out of a coconut is somewhat of an ordeal, but a satisfying one (see box, opposite). For the recipe given here, the coconut is puréed, so don't worry about grating it. Just cut it into manageable pieces—about 1 inch on each side. When grated, a coconut yields about 3 cups—more than you'll usually need—but it freezes well. This recipe is inspired by one in Madhur Jaffrey's excellent book* Flavors of India.

If you're using fresh coconut chunks, purée/chop them in a food processor. Combine the chopped or grated coconut with the cilantro, ginger, garlic, chiles, lemon juice, spices, and sugar in a blender and add the coconut milk. Purée for 3 minutes on high speed. Work the mixture through a coarse strainer or food mill to extract the liquid. Discard the solids that don't go through. Combine with the onion and season with salt to taste.

How to Get the Flesh out of a Coconut

When buying a coconut, hold it up to your ear and move it back and forth—you should hear liquid sloshing around inside. This is not coconut milk but is tasty in its own right, if a little insipid. When you get the coconut home, use a hammer and a sharpening steel to make two holes near the end of the coconut where you see little round dark spots. These spots are softer and easier to penetrate. When you've made the holes, drain out the liquid—drink it if you like—and put the coconut in a 300°F oven. (If you put the coconut in the oven without making the holes it can explode.) Bake for 15 minutes. This causes the coconut flesh to contract and pull away from the outer husk. Take it out of the oven and let cool, then go at it with a hammer to break it into two or more pieces. You should be able to see a space between the flesh and the husk. Slide a screwdriver down into this space and wedge out the flesh. The pieces of flesh are coated with a thin dark skin, which you can peel off with a vegetable peeler. The flesh is now ready for grating. You can use the grater attachment of a food processor but grating by hand with a fairly fine grater works better.

Chlorophyll for Coloring Sauces

MAKES: 2 tablespoons (1 teaspoon is needed to color 1 cup Basic Mayonnaise)

You can give your mayonnaise a green hue by using Maille brand herb mustard, which is green, or you can extract the chlorophyll from spinach and use that.

3 tightly packed cups spinach leaves (from about 10 ounces fresh spinach)

1 ½ cups cold water

about ¼ cup olive oil for storage

Put the spinach in a blender with the water. Purée for 1 minute. Strain through a strainer lined with a triple layer of cheesecloth. Discard what doesn't go through the cheesecloth. Line the strainer with a coffee filter or a paper towel. Put the liquid that went through the cheesecloth in a small saucepan over medium heat. Watch closely and wait for the moment when the green in the liquid coagulates into little pieces, about 2 minutes. Immediately strain through the coffee filter. Let it take its time—don't push down on it—and use a spoon to scoop out what doesn't go through the cloth. This is the pure chlorophyll. Use it in small amounts to color cold sauces. To save what you don't use, put the chlorophyll in a small ramekin or jar and add enough oil to cover the surface of the chlorophyll. Keep refrigerated for up to 5 days.

Shrimp Butter

MAKES ⅓ pound

This bright orange, flavorful butter is used to finish warm sauces, such as the Sauce Crevettes *on page 173. It can also be stirred into soups just before serving to provide color and flavor.*

Make sure the shrimp heads and butter are well chilled. Cut the butter into 4 chunks and combine it with the heads in the bowl of a stand mixer fitted with the paddle blade. Turn the mixer on low. At the beginning the heads may try to escape but as the blade breaks them up you'll be able to gradually increase the speed to medium. Leave on medium speed for 20 minutes. At this point there will be a mess in the mixer—a bunch of broken up shells coated with pink butter. Transfer this mixture to a saucepan over low heat. Cook over low heat for 30 minutes. If at any point the butter begins to sizzle, turn down the heat. Add 1½ cups of water to the mixture in the saucepan—or more as needed to completely cover the heads—and bring back to a simmer. Let cool at room temperature for an hour and transfer to the refrigerator. Chill overnight. Use a spoon to remove the congealed layer of orange butter that's formed on top. Discard the shells and water. Melt the butter in a small saucepan and strain it through a fine-mesh strainer. The shrimp butter will keep for weeks in the refrigerator or for months in the freezer, tightly covered.

1 pound (about 1 quart) shrimp heads or 3 quarts shrimp shells

½ cup (1 stick) butter

conversions

volume equivalents

These are not exact equivalents for American cups and spoons, but have been rounded up or down slightly to make measuring easier.

AMERICAN	METRIC	IMPERIAL
¼ t	1.2 ml	
½ t	2.5 ml	
1 t	5.0 ml	
½ T (1.5 t)	7.5 ml	
1 T (3 t)	15 ml	
¼ cup (4 T)	60 ml	2 fl oz
⅓ cup (5 T)	75 ml	2½ fl oz
½ cup (8 T)	125 ml	4 fl oz
⅔ cup (10 T)	150 ml	5 fl oz
¾ cup (12 T)	175 ml	6 fl oz
1 cup (16 T)	250 ml	8 fl oz
1 ¼ cups	300 ml	10 fl oz (½ pint)
1 ½ cups	350 ml	12 fl oz
2 cups (1 pint)	500 ml	16 fl oz
2 ½ cups	625 ml	20 fl oz (1 pint)
1 quart	1 liter	32 fl oz

oven temperature equivalents

OVEN MARK	F	C	GAS
Very cool	250–275	130–140	½–1
Cool	300	150	2
Warm	325	170	3
Moderate	350	180	4
Moderately hot	375	190	5
	400	200	6
Hot	425	220	7
	450	230	8
Very hot	475	250	9

weight equivalents

The metric weights given in this chart are not exact equivalents, but have been rounded up or down slightly to make measuring easier.

AVOIRDUPOIS	METRIC
¼ oz	7 g
½ oz	15 g
1 oz	30 g
2 oz	60 g
3 oz	90 g
4 oz	115 g
5 oz	150 g
6 oz	175 g
7 oz	200 g
8 oz (½ lb)	225 g
9 oz	250 g
10 oz	300 g
11 oz	325 g
12 oz	350 g
13 oz	375 g
14 oz	400 g
15 oz	425 g
16 oz (1 lb)	450 g
1 ½ lb	750 g
2 lb	900 g
2 ¼ lb	1 kg
3 lb	1.4 kg
4 lb	1.8 kg

acknowledgments

WHILE *SIMPLY SHRIMP* IS NOT A HUGE BOOK, it represents an enormous effort by a small group of dedicated people. Particularly amazing is the versatility of all the members of the team who worked as assistants, food stylists, cooks, recipe testers, editors, and bookkeepers. Denise Michelson did most of the work and put together a team as well as helped style many of the shots. Iri Snow Greco and Rebecca Jurkevich also helped cook beautiful food and style photographs. Laurie Knoop and Miranda Kany oversaw much of the text and the recipe testing. I'd also like to thank those at Stewart, Tabori & Chang, especially my editor Leslie Stoker for her optimism and encouragement, and Chris Gardner for her hard work putting together the final galleys and overseeing the final editing. Thanks to the guys at Fish Tales in Brooklyn, New York for being so attentive to even my most bizarre request. Deepest thanks to my agents Elise and Arnold Goodman for being there for me and for being much more than agents and last, to my partner, Zelik, for putting up with shrimp everywhere and for being shrimp tester par excellence.

index